TREES

A Quick Reference Guide
to Trees
of North America

by
Robert H. Mohlenbrock
and
John W. Thieret

COLLIER BOOKS
Macmillan Publishing Company, New York
Collier Macmillan Publishers, London

On the cover: Black oak, *Quercus velutina;*
                    Shumard oak, *Quercus shumardii* (page 66).
Color illustrations by Howard S. Friedman.

Species range maps drawn by Ruth Adam.
Black-and-white illustrations of tree and leaf shapes by Mark Mohlenbrock.

Copyright © 1987 by Macmillan Publishing Company,
a division of Macmillan, Inc.

Macmillan Publishing Company
866 Third Avenue, New York, N.Y. 10022
Collier Macmillan Canada, Inc.

Library of Congress Cataloging-in-Publication Data

Mohlenbrock, Robert H., 1931–
    Trees : a quick reference guide to trees of North America.

    (Macmillan field guides)
    Includes index.
    1. Trees—United States—Identification. 2. Trees—
Canada—Identification. I. Thieret, John W.
II. Title. III. Series.
QK115.M57   1987   582.160973   87-11712

ISBN 0-02-063430-7

10 9 8 7 6 5 4 3 2 1

The Macmillan Field Guide Series: Trees is also published
in a hardcover edition by Macmillan Publishing Company.

Printed in the United States of America

Acknowledgments

The authors gratefully acknowledge the assistance given them in the field for several years by their families—Beverly, Mark, Wendy, and Trent Mohlenbrock and Mildred, Richard, and Jeffrey Thieret. Matthew Hils and David M. Brandenburg helped during field trips made to gather data for the conifer section of the book. The authors wish to express their deepest appreciation to Michael Agnes, their editor at Macmillan, for his meticulous effort in putting this book together.

Robert H. Mohlenbrock
John W. Thieret

Contents

Introduction

This is a tree identification book. It is meant for persons who know little about trees but are interested in finding out more about them. It will help them learn tree names if they are willing to give to the pursuit the effort it deserves—Nature gives away few of her secrets to those unwilling to strive for them. Identification of a tree as a member of a particular genus— i.e., as one of the firs, the pines, the oaks, the ashes—is usually not much of a challenge, but identification of an individual species—i.e., the *kind* of fir, pine, juniper, oak, ash—is often less easy. Indeed, in some cases it may be impossible for anyone but a person with considerable experience in tree identification.

At the heart of the book are the color plates of trees and the descriptions facing the plates. These have been designed with the novice in mind, but they can be valuable to anyone studying trees. Used carefully, the book should open to you the world of tree identification. However, we hope that learning just a tree's name will not be sufficient to satisfy your curiosity. Don't stop there! Once you know the name, you have the key that will unlock further information about the bearer of the name. You will be able to look it up in the great number of volumes devoted in whole or in part to trees. Our book, then, should start you on the road to knowledge of trees.

The area covered by the book is Canada and the continental United States, including Alaska but excluding southern Florida, whose tree flora is so different from the rest of the United States that it deserves a book of its own. The guide is equally useful, then, in Nevada, North Dakota, and Nova Scotia or in the delta of the Mississippi and the delta of the Mackenzie.

The book illustrates 232 kinds of trees, or about one-third of the tree species occurring wild in North America north of Mexico. These are the ones you are most likely to see on a trip to the mountains, the seashore, or the plains; along a highway or in a fencerow during a drive in the country; on a picnic or a camping or fishing trip in a county, state, or national park or forest. Most of the trees we include are North American natives, but a few—e.g., Scots pine, Siberian elm, white willow, royal paulownia—are introduced trees that have gone wild.

The book does not purport to account for all of the many hundreds of kinds of trees that may be grown in parks, yards, arboretums, and shelterbelts. Of course, some of these are included, but only those that also occur in the wild. For example, blue spruce, white pine, American elm, flowering dogwood, green ash, and sugar and red maples—to cite but a few among many—are native North American trees common in the wild and also extensively grown in our towns and cities. They, and others like them, are in the book.

What Is a Tree?

To define a tree is not so easy as one might think. To begin with, a tree is a plant that produces wood in its stem—it is, in the parlance of the botanist, a woody plant. But trees are not the only kinds of plants that produce wood. The others are certain vines and shrubs (or bushes). The distinction between a tree and a vine poses no problem: a vine is a climbing plant, one that requires some support on which to grow. Think of the grape vines of our temperate regions or the great lianas of tropical forests.

It is the distinction between a tree and a shrub that may give us some difficulty. Of the several definitions of "tree" that have been proposed, perhaps the best for the purposes of this book is this: a tree is a woody plant that grows at least 20' tall and typically has a trunk unbranched for at least several feet above the ground and at least 4" in diameter. In contrast, a shrub is generally shorter and is "bushy" in aspect, that is, it has several or many stems arising from the base of the plant; these stems are usually less than 4" in diameter.

These arbitrary definitions "work" well enough most of the time. However, there are plants that are more or less intermediate between what people think of when they hear the word "tree" and what they think of when they hear the word "shrub." Nature does not always fit comfortably into pigeonholes that humans create. What, for example, is a young paper birch that is 12' tall and has four stems, the largest of which is 3" in diameter? Using the definitions above, we probably would call it a large shrub. But given a few more years of growth in height and stem diameter, our plant would achieve the rank of tree. Fortunately, minor problems such as this are few.

Arbitrary definitions aside, we believe that most people will know, most of the time, whether the woody plant they are looking at is a tree or a shrub.

Conifers Versus Hardwoods

Each tree in this book belongs to one of two groups. You are already familiar, at least in a general way, with both of these. The first group comprises the conifers; the second, the hardwoods, or broad-leaved trees. Botanists use the terms "gymnosperms" and "angiosperms," respectively, for these two groups.

The conifers include such well-known trees as redwood, firs, spruces, hemlocks, pines, and various cedars. The leaves of these trees are either needles or scales. Needles are examplified by those of pines and firs: they are several to many times as long as they are wide, more or less parallel-sided, flattened or 4-angled in cross section, and ¼" to 12" long, in most cases, the stems of needle-leaved trees are visible among the leaves. Scales are exemplified by those of junipers: they are mostly no more than twice as long as they are wide, more or less triangular in outline, overlapping like shingles on a roof, and ½" or less (mostly less) long; in most cases, the stems of scale-leaved trees are *not* visible among the leaves. Almost all conifers are evergreen. In most of the United States and Canada, the only green trees you are likely to see in the winter are conifers.

The seeds of most conifers are borne in cones, which are familiar to everybody. There are exceptions, however, such as the yews. Do not seek for flowers on conifers. They have none.

Trees belonging to the other group, the hardwoods, are just as easy to recognize. These are the broad-leaved trees, like oak and cottonwood. They have leaves of the kind that most people think of when they hear the word "leaf," that is, a flat, green structure growing from a twig. Most of the hardwood species in this book are deciduous, that is, they drop their leaves at the end of the growing season. A few—for example, southern magnolia, live oak, loblolly-bay, and mountain-laurel—are evergreen.

Hardwoods bear flowers. Sometimes these are showy; magnolia flowers and cherry flowers are good examples. But sometimes they are inconspicuous, so much so, in fact, that most people would not call them flowers. Oak flowers and elm flowers are in this nonshowy category.

The seeds of hardwoods are produced in fruits. To the average person, some of these fruits—acorns, for example—may not appear very fruit-like, but they *are* fruits, nonetheless; they have developed from the ovary of the flower and contain one or more seeds.

Explanation of the Plates

The plates are arranged with the conifers—needle-leaved or scale-leaved, mostly cone-bearing trees—occupying the first 17 plates. The remainder of the plates, 41 of them, present the hardwoods, almost all of which are broad-leaved trees. A quick glance through the conifer plates and then through the hardwood plates should be sufficient to familiarize you with the basic features of each of these groups. Reading the section "Conifers versus Hardwoods" in this introduction will help, too.

Within the gymnosperms, arrangement is as follows:

1. Needle-leaved trees whose needles are borne singly.
2. Needle-leaved trees whose needles are borne in bunches.
3. Scale-leaved trees whose twigs are flattened.
4. Scale-leaved trees whose twigs are more or less square or rounded in end view.

The hardwoods present a different set of challenges with respect to identification. Here, the arrangement of the trees follows the system of classification proposed by Arthur Cronquist of the New York Botanical Garden. In that system, trees considered to have the most primitive types of flowers are given first, followed by those that are regarded as having more advanced flowers. The sequence thus mirrors the supposed chronology of evolution. You will find that this arrangement will help you identify individual species as members of larger related groups within the hardwoods.

The plates ordinarily show a leaf-bearing twig and, in addition, a cone for conifers and a flower or fruit or both for hardwoods. Enlarged drawings of twig detail are included for some conifers.

Plate Descriptions

Second in importance to the plates themselves are the descriptions and the maps facing each plate. The common names and scientific names used follow, in general, the recommendations in *Checklist of United States Trees (Native and Naturalized)* by E. L. Little, Jr. (1979). Common names of trees may vary from one part of North America to another; some trees may have several to many such names. We believe that the ones used in this book are, if not always the most widely used, then the most appropriate. In each tree description are at least two categories of information. Careful study of these, with tree at hand or specimen in hand, should enable the reader to make an identification.

1. **Field Marks:** all the important characteristics—size, leaves, flowers, cones or fruits, and so on—that distinguish this tree from others. No irrelevant or confusingly detailed descriptions are included. The figures given for height (Ht.) and trunk diameter (diam.) represent average specimens. Maximum height and diameter are seldom included. Trees of such maximum sizes are generally infrequent or rare; they may even no longer exist.

2. **Habitat:** the most typical site(s) where the tree grows. It is possible, of course, that an occasional tree may be found in a habitat not mentioned; some trees can occur in a variety of habitats but are most often found in the one(s) listed. Elevation data are important, especially in the case of trees growing on mountains, where some species occur at low elevations and others are found higher up. Trees that have a wide north-south range—for example, subalpine fir—usually are found growing at lower elevations toward the north than they are farther south. This fact is recognized in the descriptions by statements like this: "elev. up to 1000' (north) to 3000'–6000' (south)." It may be assumed that trees found between the northern and southern extremes of the range will be found at intermediate elevations.

For some trees, the following additional section is included in the description.

3. **Comments:** descriptions of important variations of the tree or similar species in the same range that are not treated separately.

The maps show the overall range of each species illustrated. Knowledge of the geographic region(s) in which a tree grows is often of great value in identification. Indeed, once you think you have determined the general kind of tree you are working with—for example, a fir of some sort—you should first of all check the maps to see which firs grow where you are. If, for example, you are in Great Smoky Mountains National Park just northwest of Newfound Gap in Tennessee, you can see from the fir maps that in that region there is only one kind of fir, Fraser fir. Similarly, if you are at one of the ski resorts in the mountains near Salt Lake City, a quick check of the maps will tell you that only two firs grow there. The descriptions will help you decide which one you are looking at.

The maps show two kinds of distribution. Solid shading (for small areas) and finely dotted shading (for larger areas) indicate relatively continuous distribution within the boundaries shown. Fine diagonal lines are used to show intermittent, or discontinuous, distribution, indicating that the species is found only in *some* areas within the boundaries shown. Discontinuous distribution is often characteristic of western regions, where some species are restricted to areas of specific elevation.

No maps are given for introduced (non-native) species. These trees do not have established ranges analogous to those of native trees.

Tree Regions

The map on the following page divides North America north of Mexico into 12 regions, based primarily on the plant life that occurs in each area. Most of these regions are dominated botanically by trees, although the tundra, the deserts, and the grasslands are distinct because of their noticeable paucity of woody plants. While North American forests may be classified in different ways or in greater detail, the map provides a useful, approximate guide to the continent's major forest types.

In northern Canada and Alaska and extending beyond the Arctic Circle is the tundra, a treeless plain underlain by permafrost. The vegetation is dominated by mosses, lichens, grasses, sedges, heaths, and dwarf willows and birches. None of the trees described in this field guide lives in the tundra.

Occupying a broad zone across most of Canada and Alaska south of the tundra is the boreal coniferous forest. Most of the land in this region has been glaciated; it is filled with cold lakes, bogs, and rivers. The characteristic coniferous trees of this forest are white spruce, black spruce, tamarack, jack pine, and balsam fir. The characteristic broad-leaved trees are paper birch, quaking aspen, and balsam poplar.

The principal mountain ranges of western North America are dominated by conifers. Within this region, known as the montane coniferous forest, the kinds of trees change with elevation; often the western and eastern sides of mountains are host to different species as well, the western sides typically having more precipitation. The Coast Ranges, Cascades, and Sierra Nevada in the Pacific states and British Columbia have some of the world's most splendid softwood forests. The principal trees, not all of which occur throughout the region, include western and mountain hemlocks; Douglas-fir; Sitka spruce; silver, white, and red firs; incense-cedar; western redcedar; and lodgepole, ponderosa, western white, and sugar pines. The Coast Ranges are home also to redwood, the tallest tree species; the most massive species, giant sequoia, is found in the Sierra Nevada. Forests of the Rocky Mountains are characterized mainly by Douglas-fir; subalpine and white firs; Engelmann and blue spruces; western larch; and limber, ponderosa, and whitebark pines. Quaking aspen and black cottonwood are common hardwood species. Again, none of these is present everywhere.

The chaparral and oak woodland region of central and western California is dominated by firm-leaved evergreen shrubs of various species and by evergreen or deciduous oaks: interior live oak, canyon live oak, California black oak, and valley oak.

MAJOR TREE REGIONS OF NORTH AMERICA
NORTH OF MEXICO

A. Tundra
B. Boreal Coniferous Forest
C. Montane Coniferous Forest
D. Cool Desert and
    Pinyon-Juniper Woodland
E. Warm Desert
F. Chaparral and Oak Woodland

G. Grassland
H. Southeastern Evergreen Forest
 I. Subtropical and Tropical Forest
J. Eastern Deciduous Forest
K. Grassland and Savanna
L. Mississippi Bottomland Forest

Cool desert and pinyon-juniper woodland occupy much of Utah, Nevada, and northern Arizona. Where trees occur in this area, they usually are pinyon pines and junipers. Southward into southern Arizona, adjacent California and New Mexico, and western Texas, the climate is increasingly hot and dry, resulting in an extensive warm desert. While many cacti, including the giant saguaro, dominate the landscape, some trees are able to survive: mesquite, paloverdes, and desert ironwood.

Much of the plains of central North America, from southern Canada to western Texas, is covered by a vast grassland known as the prairie. Trees, especially cottonwoods, occur here primarily along watercourses, where moisture is more plentiful.

The southeastern evergreen forest occupies the northern part of Florida; parts of Texas, Louisiana, Mississippi, Alabama, Georgia, and the Carolinas; and the southeastern tip of Virginia. On the sandy uplands there is a preponderance of pines, while the plains along the Atlantic Ocean are dominated by live oaks, whose evergreen branches are festooned with Spanish-moss. Where shaded ravines occur, southern magnolia and American holly are common evergreen species.

The only region of North America north of Mexico where subtropical and tropical tree species are found is the southern tip of Florida. Although many kinds of trees occur in this region, they are generally unrelated to most of the trees that are found elsewhere in the United States and are therefore excluded from this book.

The eastern deciduous forest covers most of the eastern half of temperate North America. A great diversity of tree species, mostly those that drop their leaves during the winter, makes up this distinctive vegetation zone. In the moister areas, sugar maple and American beech predominate, along with yellow-poplar. In drier exposures, several different species of oaks and hickories are the most abundant trees.

Southwestern Oklahoma and central Texas are home to a restricted plant habitat where grasslands and patches of forest intermingle. This area is referred to as the grassland and savanna region. Common tree species found here include post oak and blackjack oak.

Along the Mississippi River from Louisiana as far north as southern Illinois is a vegetation region we call the Mississippi bottomland forest. In swamps, where water stands all the year, baldcypress and water tupelo are the primary trees. Where water saturates the soil but does not stand throughout the year, overcup oak, willow oak, Nuttall oak, and pecan are common.

Sequence of Plates

Conifers

Hardwoods

CALIFORNIA TORREYA, PACIFIC YEW, REDWOOD, BALDCYPRESS

Needles flat, pointed, borne singly.

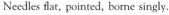

California Torreya, *Torreya californica*

Field Marks: Evergreen; needles rigid, needle-pointed, in flat to broadly V-shaped sprays, 1″–2¾″ long, with strong "piney" odor when crushed, with two narrow, pale "stripes" and three broad, darker ones below, continuing down the green twigs. Ht. 15′–90′; diam. ½′–3′. **Habitat:** Moist, wooded canyons, gulches, and coves; elev. up to 6500′.

Pacific Yew, *Taxus brevifolia*

Field Marks: Evergreen; needles mostly in flat or V-shaped sprays, not sharp to the touch, stalked (stalk ¹⁄₁₆″ long), glossy and dark green above, dull and paler green with a narrow, slightly darker border below, ³⁄₈″–1⅛″ long, continuing down the green twigs; bark thin, rough, peeling, dark purplish brown or reddish brown to salmon. Ht. 20′–60′; diam. 1′–2′. **Habitat:** Moist forests; elev. up to 7000′.

Redwood, *Sequoia sempervirens*

Field Marks: Evergreen; the tallest tree species; leaves continuing down the twigs, not stalked, of two kinds: the most obvious ones on lower branches needle-like, in flat sprays, ¼″–1¼″ long, whitish below; others mostly shorter (to ⅛″ long), even scale-like, arranged all around, and often pressed to, the twigs; bark furrowed, cinnamon-brown. Ht. 200′–275′; diam. 3′–12′. **Habitat:** Coastal forests in fog belt; elev. up to 3000′.

Baldcypress, *Taxodium distichum*

Field Marks: Deciduous; trunk base buttressed; conical "knees" up to 6′ tall often arising from the roots; needles alternate, in feather-like sprays, ¼″–¾″ long; twigs falling with needles attached. Ht. 100′ 120′; diam. 3′–5′. **Habitat:** Swamps, bottomlands. **Comment:** Pondcypress (*T. d.* var. *nutans*), of wet areas from Va. to Fla. and La., differs in having smaller, scale-like to needle-like leaves arranged all around, and pressed to, the twigs.

California Torreya

bottom

top

Pacific Yew

bottom

top

Redwood

top

bottom

Baldcypress

Pondcypress
close-up of twig

FIRS

Evergreens. Needles blunt, flattened, single. The oval to round scars left after needle fall are more or less flush with the twig surface. Fir cones are on top branches and break up while on the tree. Thus, unless cut down by animals, *whole* cones do not fall to the ground; cone *scales*, though, may litter it.

The firs below have needles that are glossy green *above* but with alternating green and whitish stripes *below* (the whitish stripes are lines of minute white dots). Thus the two sides are strikingly different. The needles described are those of the lowest branches.

Fraser Fir, *Abies fraseri*
Field Marks: The only fir in its range. Ht. 30′–40′; diam. 1′–2½′. **Habitat:** Mountain forests; elev. 4000′–6600′.

Balsam Fir, *Abies balsamea*
Field Marks: The only fir in its range *east of Alberta;* needles in flat or V-shaped sprays (or, at least, with most of the needles sticking out from opposite sides of the twig), the spray, in end view, looking somewhat like a bow tie. Ht. 30′–60′; diam. 1′–1½′. **Habitat:** Forests; elev. up to 5600′.

Pacific Silver Fir, *Abies amabilis*
Field Marks: Needles usually notched at the tip, with a "suction cup" base, some of them spreading horizontally, others (often shorter) pointing forward, pressed against and concealing the upper side of the twigs; cones purple. Ht. 140′–160′; diam. 2′–4′. **Habitat:** Coniferous forests; elev. up to 1000′ (north) to 1000′–6000′ (south).

Grand Fir, *Abies grandis*
Field Marks: Needles often notched at the tip, with a "suction cup" base, in flat or V-shaped sprays, *not* concealing the upper side of the twigs; cones yellow-green. Ht. 50′–200′; diam. 1′–4′. **Habitat:** Coniferous forests; elev. up to 7000′.

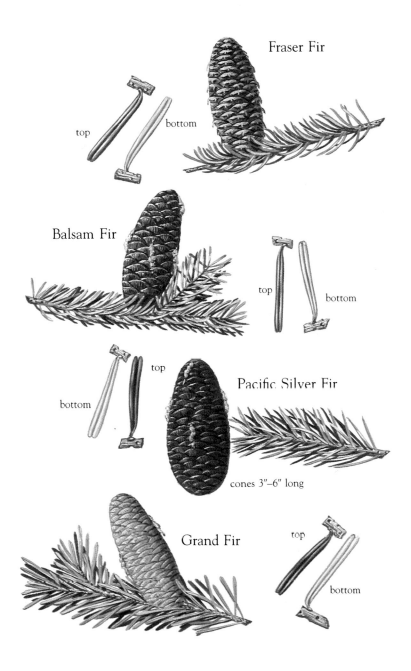

Fraser Fir

top
bottom

Balsam Fir

top
bottom

bottom
top

Pacific Silver Fir

cones 3″–6″ long

top
bottom

Grand Fir

FIRS

Evergreens. Needles blunt, flattened, single. The oval to round scars left after needle fall are more or less flush with the twig surface. Fir cones are on top branches and break up while on the tree. Thus, unless cut down by animals, *whole* cones do not fall to the ground; cone *scales*, though, may litter it.

The firs below have needles with green and whitish stripes (sometimes faint) on *both* sides. The needles described are those of the lowest branches.

To see resin ducts, cut an older needle (one far back on a branch) in two or pull it apart; examine an exposed surface with a hand lens.

Subalpine Fir, *Abies lasiocarpa*

Field Marks: Young needles grooved above, with a "suction cup" base; resin ducts obvious, each a tiny eye near the midvein; 1-year-old twigs hairy. Ht. 60′–100′; diam. 1½′–2′. **Habitat:** Mountain forests; elev. up to 3500′ (north) to 8000′–12,000′ (south).

White Fir, *Abies concolor*

Field Marks: Needles 1″–3″ long, with a "suction cup" base, dull pale blue-green, in flat sprays or mostly pointing up (like toothbrush bristles); resin ducts hardly noticeable; 1-year-old twigs hairless. Ht. 60′–180′; diam. 1′–5′. **Habitat:** Mountain forests; elev. 3000′–11,000′.

California Red Fir, *Abies magnifica*

Field Marks: Needles ⅝″–1¼″ long, ridged above and below, 4-angled in end view, pointing up (like toothbrush bristles); needle base not narrowed, pointing forward, the rest of the needle curving out; resin ducts hardly noticeable. Ht. 60′–180′; diam. 1′–5′. **Habitat:** Mountain forests; elev. 4500′–9000′. **Comment:** The cone shown for this fir is of the Shasta variety of the species, distinctive because its bracts (pointed, papery structures) stick out beyond the cone scales; the bracts of typical red fir do not so protrude.

Noble Fir, *Abies procera*

Field Marks: Needles ¾″–1½″ long, grooved above, ridged below, pointing up (like toothbrush bristles); needle base not narrowed, pointing forward, the rest of the needle curving out; resin ducts hardly noticeable; 1-year-old twigs hairy. Ht. 80′–200′; diam. 2′–6′. **Habitat:** Mountain forests; elev. 1500′–6000′.

Subalpine Fir

top

bottom

White Fir

top

bottom

California Red Fir

top

bottom

Noble Fir

top

bottom

DOUGLAS-FIR, HEMLOCKS

Douglas-fir, *Pseudotsuga menziesii*

Field Marks: Evergreen; cones 2″–4½″ long, falling at maturity, with 3-pointed bracts (papery structures) among the scales; needles radiating in all directions from the twigs (like a bottle brush), flat, stalked, blunt to pointed, borne singly, with green and whitish stripes below (note younger leaves); leaf scars a bit wider than long, tilted, flush with the twig on the upper side, slightly raised on the lower. Ht. 80′–200′; diam. 2′–6′. **Habitat:** Forests; elev. up to 10,000′. **Comments:** Bigcone Douglas-fir (*P. macrocarpa*), of mountains of s. Calif., has larger cones (3¾″–7½″ long).

Hemlocks: Evergreens; needles flat, blunt, stalked (stalk parallel to the twig), borne singly on "pegs" about ⅓₂″ long; "pegs" lying against the twigs and remaining after leaf fall.

Eastern Hemlock, *Tsuga canadensis*

Field Marks: Needles white-striped below, with fine teeth on the edge, in flat sprays; cones ½″–¾″ long, the scales circular. Ht. 60′–100′; diam. 1½′–4′. **Habitat:** Swamp borders, forests, rock outcrops; elev. up to 5000′. **Comments:** Carolina hemlock (*T. caroliniana*), of mountain forests from s.w. Va. to n.e. Ga., has smooth-edged leaves *not* in flat sprays and cones ¾″–1½″ long with *oval* scales.

Mountain Hemlock, *Tsuga mertensiana*

Field Marks: Needles with two faint stripes on each surface, dull blue-green, radiating in all directions from the twigs; cones ¾″–3″ long. Ht. 50′–100′; diam. 10″–30″. **Habitat:** Coniferous forests; elev. up to 3000′ (north) to 6000′–11,000′ (south).

Western Hemlock, *Tsuga heterophylla*

Field Marks: Needles white-striped below, glossy green above, forming flat sprays; sometimes a few short needles lying, striped side up, against and parallel to the upper side of the twigs; cones ⅝″–1″ long. Ht. 100′–175′; diam. 2′–4′. **Habitat:** Coniferous forests; elev. up to 3000′ (north) or 6000′ (south).

Douglas-fir

Eastern Hemlock

top

bottom

top

bottom

Mountain Hemlock

top

bottom

Western Hemlock

SPRUCES

Evergreens. Needles borne singly on "pegs" about 1/32" long; "pegs" stick out from the twigs and remain, stubble-like, after needle fall. Identification may be easier if cones are present.

Sitka Spruce, *Picea sitchensis*
Field Marks: One of two North American native spruces with flat needles; twigs not hairy; cone scales with jagged edges. Ht. 125'–200', diam. 4'–6'. **Habitat:** Coastal forests; elev. up to 1200' (rarely 3900'). **Comment:** The other flat-needled North American spruce is Brewer spruce (*P. brewerana*), of the mountains of s.w. Ore. and n.w. Calif. It has hairy twigs and smooth-edged cone scales.

Red Spruce, *Picea rubens*
Field Marks: Twigs finely hairy; needles square in end view, yellow-green; cones 1"–2" long, falling when mature, with scales smooth-edged to jagged-edged. Ht. 50'–70'; diam. 1'–2'. **Habitat:** Forests, rocky slopes; elev. up to 6500'.

Black Spruce, *Picea mariana*
Field Marks: Twigs finely hairy; needles square in end view, blue-green; cones 1/2"–1 1/2" long, often remaining in dense bunches on upper branches for years, the scales usually jagged-edged. Ht. 10'–60'; diam. 1/2'–1 1/2'. **Habitat:** Bogs and bottomlands to dry rocky slopes; elev. up to 5000'.

White Spruce, *Picea glauca*
Field Marks: Twigs not hairy; needles square in end view; cones 1"–2 1/2" long, falling soon after maturity, with scales rounded to nearly straight, smooth-edged. Ht. 40'–110'; diam. 1 1/2'–2'. **Habitat:** Forests; elev. up to 5000'.

Sitka Spruce

cross section of needle

Red Spruce

cross section of needle

Black Spruce

cross section of needle

White Spruce

cross section of needle

SPRUCES, LARCHES

Spruces: Evergreens. Needles borne singly on "pegs" about ¹⁄₃₂″ long; "pegs" stick out from the twigs and remain, stubble-like, after needle fall.

Engelmann Spruce, *Picea engelmannii*

Field Marks: Twigs usually hairy; needles angled forward, square in end view, flexible, not especially sharp, with a disagreeable odor when crushed; cones 1″–3″ long, with scales wedge-shaped and jagged-edged. Ht. 100′–120′; diam. 1½′–2½′. **Habitat:** Mountain coniferous forests; elev. from 1000′ (north) and 10,000′ (south) to timberline (4000′–12,000′).

Blue Spruce, *Picea pungens*

Field Marks: Twigs hairless; needles almost at right angles to the twig, square in end view, stiff, very sharp; cones 2½″–4½″ long, with scales wedge-shaped and jagged-edged. Ht. 70′–90′; diam. 1½′–3′. **Habitat:** Mountain coniferous forests; elev. 6000′–11,000′.

Larches: Deciduous. Needles in brush-like clusters of 12–40 on short stubs along the branchlets.

Tamarack (Eastern Larch), *Larix laricina*

Field Marks: The only native larch in its range; cones ³⁄₈″–¾″ long, with 10–20 scales. Ht. 10′–80′; diam. ¼′–2′. **Habitat:** Swamps, bogs, floodplains, uplands; elev. up to 4000′. **Comment:** European larch (*L. decidua*)—cones ¾″–1½″ long, with 40–50 scales—may spread from cultivation in n.e. U.S.

Western Larch, *Larix occidentalis*

Field Marks: Twigs hairy at first, later hairless; needles 3-angled in end view. Ht. 100′–180′; diam. 3′–4′. **Habitat:** Mountain forests; elev. 1800′–7000′. **Comment:** Subalpine larch (*L. lyallii*) has densely white-woolly twigs and needles that are 4-angled in end view; it grows at or near timberline in British Columbia, Alberta, Wash., and Mont.

Engelmann Spruce

cross section of needle

Blue Spruce

cross section of needle

Tamarack
(Eastern Larch)

Western Larch

5-NEEDLE PINES

5-needle pines *without* prickles on cone scales; a "scar" at the very tip of each scale.

To determine if a pine needle is rough-edged, rub it lightly, from the tip down, between your thumb and index finger; if it is rough-edged, you will feel a slight roughness.

Eastern White Pine, *Pinus strobus*
Field Marks: The only native 5-needle pine in its range. Ht. 80'–175'; diam. 2'–5'. **Habitat:** Forests, dry ridges, wet areas; elev. up to 4000'.

Western White Pine, *Pinus monticola*
Field Marks: Needles 1¼"–4" long, blue-green, white-lined on inner surfaces only, sometimes rough-edged, not sharp-tipped; cones 5"–15" long, with a stalk 1" long or less; seed wing longer than the seed, leaving an imprint on the cone scale. Ht. 45'–130'; diam. 2'–6'. **Habitat:** Forests; elev. up to 9800'.

Sugar Pine, *Pinus lambertiana*
Field Marks: Needles 2½"–4" long, white-lined on all surfaces, rough-edged, sharp-tipped; cones 10"–26" long, with a stalk 1½"–4" long; seed wing longer than the seed, leaving an imprint on the cone scale. Ht. 100'–160'; diam. 2'–6'. **Habitat:** Mountain forests; elev. 1000'–10,500'.

Limber Pine, *Pinus flexilis*
Field Marks: Needles 1½"–3½" long, smooth-edged; cones 2½"–10" long, yellow-brown, opening when mature, with a stalk less than ½" long; seed wing vestigial (no imprint on cone scale). Ht. 25'–50'; diam. 1'–3'. **Habitat:** Dry slopes and ridges; elev. 7500'–12,000'. **Comments:** Southwestern white pine (*P. strobiformis*), of mountains from w. Texas to central N.M. and central Ariz., is similar, but the tips of its cone scales curve backward. Whitebark pine (*P. albicaulis*), of high elevations from British Columbia and Alberta south to Mont., Calif., Nev., Ida., and Wyo., is also similar; its cones, with deep red to purplish scales, do not open when mature but release their seeds through decay.

Eastern White Pine

cones 4″–9″ long

Western White Pine

cones 5″–15″ long

Sugar Pine

cones 10″–26″ long

cones 2½″–10″ long

Limber Pine

5-NEEDLE PINES, PINYON PINES

5-needle pines *with* prickles on cone scales.

Colorado Bristlecone Pine, *Pinus aristata*

Field Marks: Leaves ¾"–1½" long, pointing forward, densely clothing the branches, with whitish dots of resin on the surface. Ht. 20'–40'; diam. 1'–2½'. **Habitat:** Dry rocky ridges and slopes in high mountains; elev. 7500'–11,500'.

Intermountain Bristlecone Pine,
Pinus longaeva

Field Marks: Leaves 1"–1½" long, pointing forward, densely clothing the branches. Ht. 20'–50'; diam. 1'–3'. **Habitat:** Exposed ridges and slopes in high mountains; elev. 7500'–11,500'. **Comments:** Another 5-needle pine with prickles on its cone scales is Arizona pine (*P. ponderosa arizonica*), a variety of ponderosa pine; it occurs in mountains of s.w. N.M. and s.e. Ariz.

Pinyon pines: Evergreens. Low, round-topped or flat-topped, short-trunked, even shrubby pines of dry w. and s.w. U.S. plains, foothills, mesas, ridges, and rocky places from 3500'–9000'. The needles are borne singly or in twos or threes; the base sheaths soon fall away. The cones, when open, are egg-shaped to spherical or even wider than they are long; they have no—or only minute—prickles on their scales; each scale has a "scar" back from its tip. Only the 3–15 large middle scales bear seeds (pine nuts), which are large, wingless, and edible and borne in obvious concavities.

Singleleaf Pinyon, *Pinus monophylla*

Field Marks: The only North American pine with needles mostly borne singly; needles stiff, cylindrical, sharp-pointed, 1¼"–2¼" long; cones 2"–3½" long. Ht. 15'–40'; diam. 1'–3'.

Pinyon, *Pinus edulis*

Field Marks: Needles mostly in twos, ⅞"–1¾" long; cones ¾"–2" long. Ht. 10'–35'; diam. 1'–3'. **Comments:** Mexican pinyon (*P. cembroides*), growing from central Texas to s.e. Ariz., has needles mostly in threes.

Colorado Bristlecone Pine

resin droplets on needles

cones 2″–4″ long

Intermountain Bristlecone Pine

cones 2½″–5″ long

Singleleaf Pinyon

Pinyon

EASTERN 2-NEEDLE PINES

Table-mountain Pine, *Pinus pungens*

Field Marks: Needles mostly in twos, 1½″–3½″ long; cones 2″–3½″ long, egg-shaped to spherical, persisting on the tree, each scale with a stout, sharp "claw" ⅛″–¼″ long and wide, and a mahogany red band behind the glossy brown scale-tip. Ht. 20′-70′; diam. 1′–3′. **Habitat:** Dry slopes and ridges, tablelands, old fields, mostly in mountains; elev. up to 4500′.

Sand Pine, *Pinus clausa*

Field Marks: Needles in twos, 2″–4½″ long; twigs, and branches to at least 2″ in diameter, smooth (except for leaf scars), gray; cones 2″–4″ long, broadly egg-shaped, persisting on the tree (open or not), the cone base even becoming embedded in the growing branch, each scale with a short spine. Ht. 25′–75′; diam. 1′–1½′. **Habitat:** Forests on dry, white sand, with palmettos and evergreen oaks.

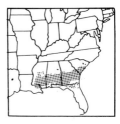

Spruce Pine, *Pinus glabra*

Field Marks: Needles in twos, 1½″–4″ long, mostly twisted; twigs, and branches to at least 2″ in diameter, smooth (except for leaf scars), gray; cones 1″–3″ long, egg-shaped, opening at maturity but staying on the tree for several years, each scale with a weak prickle or none at all. Ht. 80′–100′; diam. 1½–2½′. **Habitat:** Low moist forests along rivers and on hammocks and bottomlands, often with beech and magnolias.

Shortleaf Pine, *Pinus echinata*

Field Marks: Needles in twos or a few in threes, 2″–5″ long; twigs, and branches to at least 1″ in diameter, rough-scaly, gray-brown, peeling to show orange-tinged inner bark; cones 1¼″–3″ long, egg-shaped, opening at maturity but staying on the tree for several years, each scale with a weak prickle or none at all. Ht. 70′–100′; diam. 1½′–3′. **Habitat:** Dry uplands, old fields, forests, fencerows.

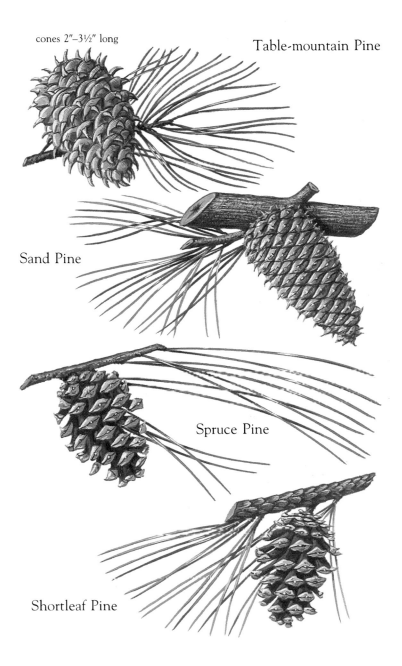

cones 2″–3½″ long

Table-mountain Pine

Sand Pine

Spruce Pine

Shortleaf Pine

EASTERN 2-NEEDLE PINES

Jack Pine, *Pinus banksiana*

Field Marks: Bark of upper trunk gray to black; needles ¾″–1½″ long; cones 1″–2″ long, curved, pointing forward, often persisting unopened on the tree, their scales with minute prickles or none at all. Ht. 20′–80′; diam. ½″–1½″. **Habitat:** Forests, sandy areas, rock outcrops; elev. 100′–2000′.

Scots Pine, *Pinus sylvestris*

Field Marks: Bark of upper trunk flaky, orange-brown to yellow-brown; needles 1½″–4″ long, often bluish green; cones 1″–2½″ long, at right angle to stem or pointing backward, opening and dropping when mature, the scales often with a minute prickle. Ht. 20′–90′; diam. 1′–3′. **Habitat:** An introduced species, now found in forests; much planted, often appearing wild, sometimes actually so.

Virginia Pine, *Pinus virginiana*

Field Marks: Needles 1½″–3″ long; bark of twigs and branches to at least 1″ in diameter more or less smooth (except for leaf scars); cones 1½″–3″ long, opening at maturity and often persisting on branches so that the tree appears full of them; cone scales with a slender prickle; youngest twigs green, later brown, usually with a waxy purplish coating, finally becoming gray-brown. Ht. 20′–60′; diam. 1″–1½″. **Habitat:** Forests, old fields, roadsides.

Red Pine, *Pinus resinosa*

Field Marks: Needles 4″–6½″ long, breaking cleanly when bent sharply; cones 1½″–2½″ long, symmetrical, at right angle to stem, their scales without prickles, with a few basal scales usually left on stem when the cone falls. Ht. 50′–80′; diam. 1′–3′. **Habitat:** Forests. **Comment:** The similar Austrian pine (*P. nigra*), a Eurasian tree much planted, may be found seemingly wild. Its needles, 3½″ 6″ long, do not break when bent sharply; its cones, with short prickles, fall intact.

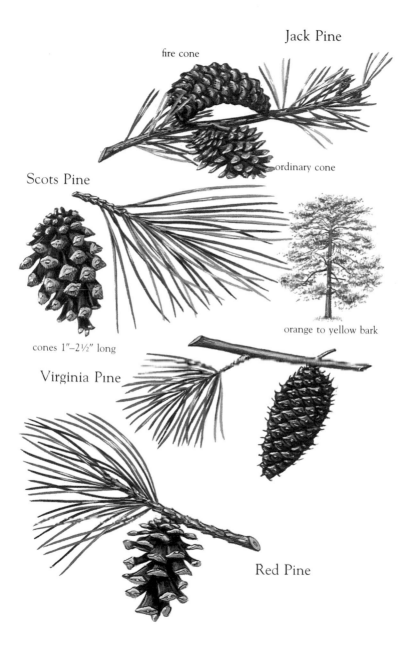

Jack Pine

fire cone

ordinary cone

Scots Pine

orange to yellow bark

cones 1"–2½" long

Virginia Pine

Red Pine

SOUTHEASTERN 2-NEEDLE AND 3-NEEDLE PINES

Longleaf Pine, *Pinus palustris*

Field Marks: Needles mostly in threes, 8″–18″ (rarely 24″) long, in fan-shaped bunches at branch tips, with sheaths ½″–1¼″ long; terminal bud wider than ½″, shaggy, silvery to grayish; twigs scaly, at least ¾″ wide; cones 5″–11″ long, at least 4″ wide when open, each scale tip with a prickle. Ht. 80′–100′; diam. 1′–3′. **Habitat:** Dryland to wetland forests.

Slash Pine, *Pinus elliottii*

Field Marks: Needles in twos and threes or mainly in twos, 5″–11″ long, with sheaths about ½″ long; terminal bud at least ¼″ wide, brownish; twigs scaly, ⅜″–½″ wide; cones 2½″–6″ long, stalked, egg-shaped when open, with glossy brown scale tips (as if varnished), each scale tip with a prickle. Ht. 60′–100′; diam. 1′–3′. **Habitat:** Lowland to upland forests, old fields.

Loblolly Pine, *Pinus taeda*

Field Marks: Needles in threes, 5″–9″ long, with sheaths ¼″–½″ long; terminal bud at least ¼″ wide, brownish; twigs scaly; cones 3″–6″ long, not stalked, egg-shaped when open, each scale tip with a prickle. Ht. 80′–120′; diam. 1′–3′. **Habitat:** Forests, old fields, cutover lands.

Pond Pine, *Pinus serotina*

Field Marks: Needles in threes (or a few in fours), 4″–8″ long; twigs scaly; trunk and main branches usually with tufts of twigs and leaves; cones 2″–3″ long, nearly round when open, many of them persisting on the tree (the tree thus seeming full of them), stalked, but the stalks—and often also the cone base—becoming buried in the expanding branch; young cone scales with a slender prickle. Ht. 40′–80′; diam. 1′–2′. **Habitat:** Swamps, low woods.

terminal bud

Longleaf Pine

cones 5"–11" long

Slash Pine

cones 2½"–6" long

Loblolly Pine

Pond Pine

cones 2"–3" long

Coulter Pine, *Pinus coulteri*

Field Marks: Needles in threes, 6″–12″ long, bluish green; cones 9″–14″ long, heavy, scales yellow-brown, each ending in a prominent stout "claw" ½″–1½″ long; seed wing longer than the seed body. Ht. 40′–60′; diam. 1′–3′. **Habitat:** Dry to moist, rocky slopes and ridges; elev. 1000′–7000′.

Digger Pine, *Pinus sabiniana*

Field Marks: Needles in threes, 7″–13″ long, gray-green, drooping, sparse; cones 6″–10″ long, scales brown, each ending in a prominent, stout, more or less triangular "claw"; seed wing shorter than the seed body. Ht. 40′–70′; diam. 1′–2′. **Habitat:** Foothills and mountain slopes; elev. 500′–4000′.

Ponderosa Pine, *Pinus ponderosa*

Field Marks: Needles in twos and threes, 4″–11″ long, yellow-green, very faintly white-lined, often tufted at the branch tips, twigs with the odor of turpentine when crushed, brownish green when young; cones 2″–6″ long, often clustered, dropping at maturity (usually leaving a few basal scales on the twig), each scale with a usually slightly out-turned prickle. Ht. 60′–130′; diam. 2′–4′. **Habitat:** Forests; elev. up to 10,000′.

Jeffrey Pine, *Pinus jeffreyi*

Field Marks: Needles in twos and threes, 5″–10″ long, gray-green to blue-green, clearly white-lined; twigs often with the odor of lemon or citronella when crushed, purplish when young; cones 5″–15″ long, dropping at maturity (usually leaving a few basal scales on the twig), each scale with a usually slightly in-turned prickle. Ht. 60′–150′; diam. 1½′–4′. **Habitat:** Forests on mountain slopes, flats, and along streams, elev. 3500′–10,000′.

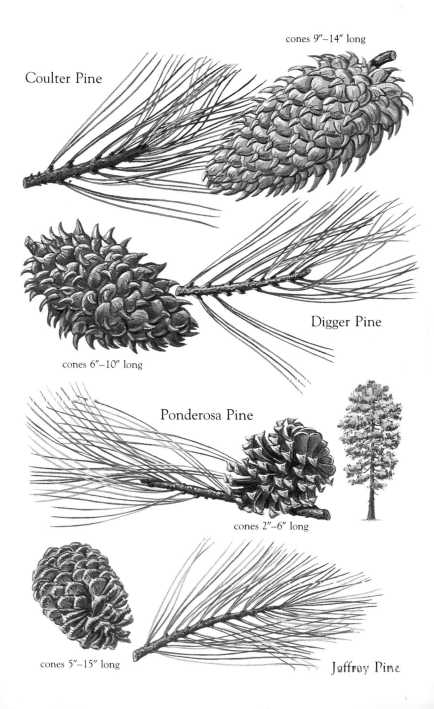

Coulter Pine

cones 9"–14" long

cones 6"–10" long

Digger Pine

Ponderosa Pine

cones 2"–6" long

cones 5"–15" long

Jeffrey Pine

WESTERN PINES, GIANT SEQUOIA

Knobcone Pine, *Pinus attenuata*

Field Marks: Needles in threes, 3"–7" long; cones 3"–6" long, clustered (often in groups encircling the stem), asymmetrical, often persisting unopened on the tree, even becoming embedded in the branches, each scale on the longer (outer) side of the cone with a pyramidal or knob-shaped tip bearing a stout point that mostly wears off. Ht. 10'–50'; diam. ½'–2½'. **Habitat:** Dry rocky ridges and slopes; elev. 1000'–4500'.

Monterey Pine, *Pinus radiata*

Field Marks: Needles in twos and threes, 3"–6" long; cones 3"–7" long, clustered, asymmetrical, often persisting unopened on the tree, each scale on the longer (outer) side of the cone with a dome-like or knob-like tip and a minute prickle, the latter often wearing off. Ht. 50'–100'; diam. 1'–3'. **Habitat:** Coastal slopes, bluffs, and ridges; also widely planted; elev. up to 1000'.

Lodgepole Pine, *Pinus contorta*

Field Marks: Needles in twos, 1"–3" long, often twisted; cones ¾"–2" long, usually asymmetrical, sometimes persisting opened or unopened on the tree, each scale with a prickle (which may wear off). Ht. 20'–100' or, along the coast, gnarled and stunted; diam. 1'–2½'. **Habitat:** Mountain forests or, along the coast, beaches, dunes, and bogs; elev. up to 11,500'.

Giant Sequoia, *Sequoiadendron giganteum*

Field Marks: Huge tree, the base much enlarged and buttressed; bark reddish brown, fibrous, deeply furrowed, 1'–2' thick; leaves scale-like, alternate, the twigs round in cross-section, almost ropelike, ⅛" in diameter. Ht. 150'–275'; diam. 10'–20'. **Habitat:** Groves in canyons or on ridges; elev. 3000'–8900'.

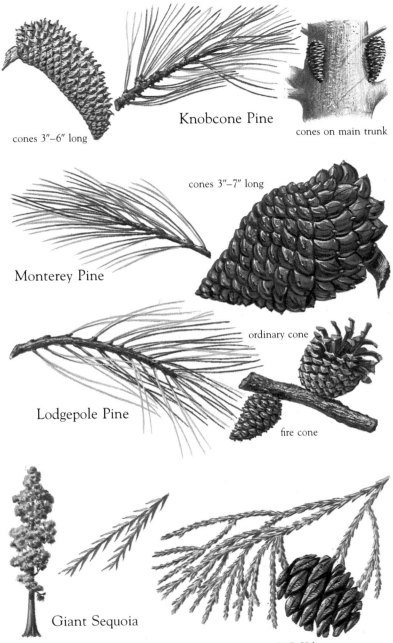

cones 3″–6″ long

Knobcone Pine

cones on main trunk

cones 3″–7″ long

Monterey Pine

ordinary cone

Lodgepole Pine

fire cone

Giant Sequoia

cones 1½″–3″ long

INCENSE-CEDAR, WHITE-CEDARS

Evergreens. Leaves scale-like, opposite, each pair at right angles to the one below, overlapping like roof shingles, the twigs more or less flattened and in flat sprays.

Incense-cedar, *Libocedrus decurrens*

Field Marks: Segments of smallest twigs mostly more than ⅛″ long, about twice or more as long as wide, vase-shaped. Ht. 60′–150′; diam. 2′–4½′. **Habitat:** Mountain forests; elev. 1200′–9000′.

Atlantic White-cedar, *Chamaecyparis thyoides*

Field Marks: Twigs less than 1/16″ wide; leaves triangular, 1/16″ long or less; cones spherical, ¼″ wide or less, opening to release seeds. Ht. 80′–100′; diam. 1′–3′. **Habitat:** Swamps, bogs, wet depressions, stream and lake shores; elev. up to 1500′.

Alaska-cedar, *Chamaecyparis nootkatensis*

Field Marks: Branches drooping; twigs about the same color on both sides, less than 1/16″ wide, twice as wide as thick, ridged in the center; leaves triangular, 1/16″–3/16″ long, the seam where the side leaves meet usually not visible, the tip of each leaf on the flat side of a twig reaching the base of the next leaf above; cones spherical, about ½″ wide, opening to release seeds. Ht. 60′–90′; diam. 2′–4′. **Habitat:** Coniferous forests; elev. up to 3000′ (north) to 2500′–7000′ (south).

Port-Orford-cedar, *Chamaecyparis lawsoniana*

Field Marks: Branches drooping; twigs often white-flecked below and sometimes above, less than 1/16″ wide; leaves triangular, about 1/16″ long, the seam where the side leaves meet usually visible, the tip of each leaf on the flat side of a twig often not reaching the base of the next leaf above; cones spherical, about ⅜″ wide, opening to release seeds. Ht. 70′–180′; diam. 2½′–6′. **Habitat:** Coastal forests; elev. up to 5000′.

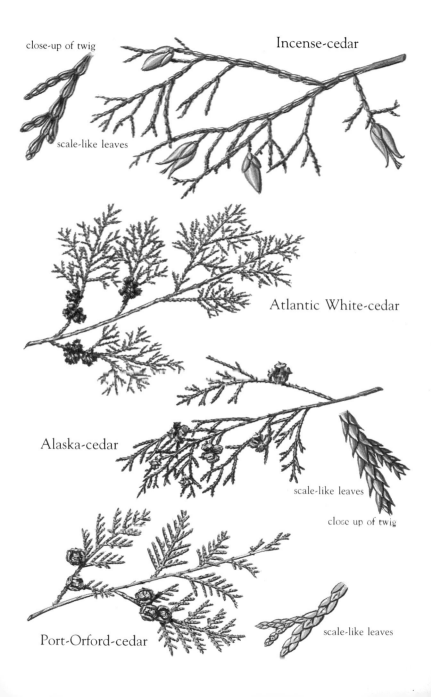

close-up of twig

scale-like leaves

Incense-cedar

Atlantic White-cedar

Alaska-cedar

scale-like leaves

close up of twig

Port-Orford-cedar

scale-like leaves

THUJAS, ARIZONA CYPRESS, EASTERN REDCEDAR

Evergreens. Leaves opposite, either scale-like (⅛" long or less) and overlapping like roof shingles or (in eastern redcedar) also needle-like (to ⅜" long).

Northern White-cedar, *Thuja occidentalis*

Field Marks: Only native thuja in its range; twigs dark green above, yellow-green below, ¹⁄₁₆" wide or more, much flattened, in flat sprays, the individual segments ⅛" long or less, curved on the edges, almost bead-like. Ht. 40'–50'; diam. 1'–3'. **Habitat:** Swampy ground, limestone outcrops; elev. up to 3000'.

Western Redcedar, *Thuja plicata*

Field Marks: Only native thuja in its range; twigs dark green above, yellow-green below, ¹⁄₁₆" wide or more, much flattened (looking almost ironed), the individual segments ⅛" long or less, curved on the edges, almost bead-like. Ht. 70'–200', diam. 2'–8'. **Habitat:** Moist sites on flats, slopes, and stream banks; elev. up to 3000' (north) or 7500' (south).

Arizona Cypress, *Cupressus arizonica*

Field Marks: Twigs square to round in end view, with a skunk-like odor if bruised, blue-green to silvery; leaves finely jagged-edged; cones spherical, ¾"–1¼" wide, hard, dark red-brown, with 6–8 scales having a central projection. Ht. 30'–80', diam. 1½'–2½'. **Habitat:** Slopes and canyons; elev. 3500'–8000'.

Eastern Redcedar, *Juniperus virginiana;*
(Including *J. v.* var. *silicicola*)

Field Marks: Trunk single, usually unbranched near the base; twigs square to rounded in end view, the leaves either scale-like (to ¹⁄₁₆" long) or needle-like (to ⅜" long) or both, their edges smooth (under 20× magnification); cones berry-like, not opening, spherical, ¼"–⅜" long, pale green turning to dark blue, with a whitish coat, with 1 or 2 blunt-tipped seeds. Ht. 25'–60'; diam. ⅔'–3'. **Habitat:** Fields, slopes, ridgetops, fencerows, rock outcrops; elev. up to 4500'.

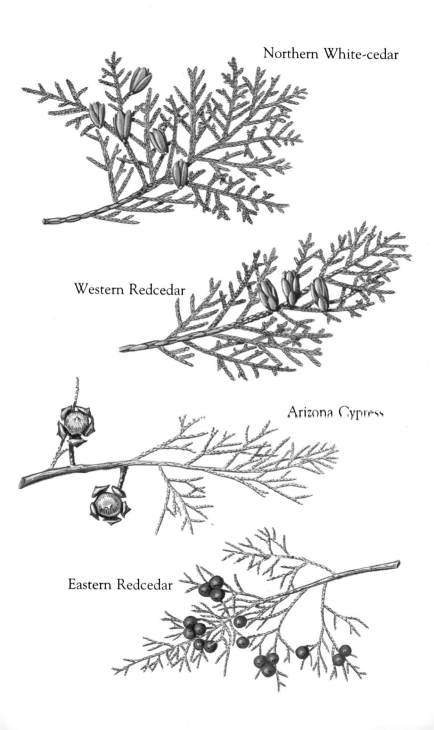

Northern White-cedar

Western Redcedar

Arizona Cypress

Eastern Redcedar

WESTERN JUNIPERS
WITH BLUISH TO BLUE-BLACK "BERRIES"

Evergreens with scale-like, triangular leaves ¹⁄₁₆″–⅛″ long and, frequently, some needle-like leaves up to ⅜″ long as well; both kinds may occur on the same plant. The twigs are square to rounded in end view. The cones, or "berries," are spherical to egg-shaped; without them, individual juniper species may be difficult or even impossible for the beginner to identify.

To check "berry" color, rub off any whitish coating that may be present.

One-seed Juniper, *Juniperus monosperma*

Field Marks: Low-branched or several-trunked tree (trunks arising at or even below ground level), rarely with a single trunk; bark scaly and shredded; twigs over ¹⁄₁₆″ wide; leaf edges minutely jagged (under 20× magnification); "berries" ⅛″–¼″ long, mostly 1-seeded. Ht. 6′–50′; diam. ½′–2′. **Habitat:** Dry slopes, plains; elev. 300′–7000′.

Rocky Mountain Juniper,
Juniperus scopulorum

Field Marks: Trunk single but sometimes branched near the base; twigs ¹⁄₁₆″ or less wide; leaf margins smooth (under 20× magnification); "berries" ¼″–⅜″ wide, mostly 2-seeded. Ht. 10′–55′; diam. ½′–2′. **Habitat:** Canyons, mountain slopes, mesas; elev. 5000′–9500′.

Ashe Juniper, *Juniperus ashei*

Field Marks: Trunk single but sometimes branched near base; twigs ¹⁄₁₆″ or less wide; leaves mostly in twos, their edges minutely jagged (under 20× magnification); "berries" ¼″–⅜″ wide, with the usually single seed sharp-tipped. Ht. 10′–40′; diam. ½′–1½′. **Habitat:** Canyons, slopes, flats; elev. 600′–2000′.

Western Juniper, *Juniperus occidentalis*

Field Marks: Trunk sometimes branched near the base; leaves in threes or sometimes in twos, with a conspicuous "dot" on the back, with edges minutely jagged (under 20× magnification); "berries" ¼″–⅓″ wide, mostly 2-seeded or 3-seeded, with a thick, tough skin. Ht. 10′–60′, diam. 1′–4′. **Habitat:** Foothills, mountain slopes, canyons, mesas; elev. 2500′–10,500′.

One-seed Juniper

close-up

Rocky Mountain Juniper

close-up

Ashe Juniper

Western Juniper

WESTERN JUNIPERS
WITH BROWNISH TO REDDISH "BERRIES"

Evergreens with scale-like, triangular leaves $\frac{1}{16}"–\frac{1}{8}"$ long and, frequently, some needle-like leaves up to $\frac{3}{8}"$ long as well; both kinds may occur on the same plant. The twigs are square to rounded in end view. The cones, or "berries," are spherical to egg-shaped; without them, individual juniper species may be difficult or even impossible for the beginner to identify.

To check "berry" color, rub off any whitish coating that may be present.

Alligator Juniper, *Juniperus deppeana*

Field Marks: Bark divided into many rectangular to square sections (like alligator hide); "berries" purplish brown or red-brown to tan, with a whitish coat. Ht. 20'–60'; diam. 1'–4'. **Habitat:** Hillsides, canyons, plateaus; elev. 4500'–8400'.

Pinchot Juniper, *Juniperus pinchotii*

Field Marks: Usually multiple-trunked, often shrubby; bark shredded; leaf edges minutely jagged (under 20× magnification); "berries" ¼" long, 1-seeded or 2-seeded, reddish brown or copper brown, without a whitish coat. Ht. 5'–20'; diam. ¼'–1'. **Habitat:** Canyons, slopes, plains; elev. 3000'–6500'.

Utah Juniper, *Juniperus osteosperma*

Field Marks: Tree single-trunked, sometimes with low branches nearly as wide as the trunk; bark shredded; twigs over $\frac{1}{16}"$ wide; leaves without visible "dots" on the back, with edges minutely jagged (under 20× magnification); "berries" ¼"–¾" long, 1-seeded or 2-seeded, brown to red-brown, with a whitish coat. Ht. 10'–40'; diam. ⅓'–3'. **Habitat:** Plains, plateaus, foothills, elev. 3000'–8500'.

California Juniper, *Juniperus californica*

Field Marks: Tree usually single-trunked; trunk deeply furrowed, sometimes with low branches; bark shredded; leaves mostly in threes; each usually with a "dot" on the back; "berries" ⅜"–¾" long, 1-seeded or 2-seeded, thin-skinned, red-brown, with a whitish coat. Ht. 10'–30'; diam. ½'–1½'. **Habitat:** Dry slopes, flats, deserts; elev. 2000'–5000'.

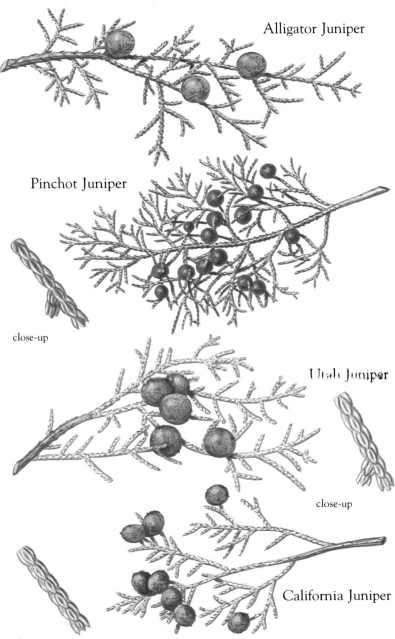

Alligator Juniper

Pinchot Juniper

close-up

Utah Juniper

close-up

California Juniper

close-up

MAGNOLIAS

Leaves alternate, simple, without teeth.

Southern Magnolia, *Magnolia grandiflora*
Field Marks: Leaves evergreen, leathery, up to 8″ long, with rusty hairs on the lower surface; flowers showy, 6″–10″ across, with 10–14 creamy white petal-like parts, fragrant; fruits cone-like, with brown hairs, 2″–3″ long, with bright red seeds. Ht. 60′–100′; diam. 2′–4½′. **Habitat:** Low woods, swamps, hammocks, around ponds.

Sweetbay, *Magnolia virginiana*
Field Marks: Leaves usually evergreen but not leathery, up to 5″ long, with silver hairs on the lower surface; flowers moderately showy, up to 5″ across, with 6–14 white petal-like parts, fragrant; fruits cone-like, pink, smooth, up to 2″ long, with dark red seeds. Ht. 30′–85′; diam. 1′–2′. **Habitat:** Swamps, low woods, near streams.

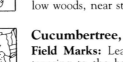

Cucumbertree, *Magnolia acuminata*
Field Marks: Leaves deciduous, up to 10″ long, tapering to the base, lower surface pale with fine hairs; flowers greenish yellow, up to 5″ across, with 9 petal-like parts, not fragrant; fruits cucumber-shaped, up to 2½″ long, red at maturity with red-orange seeds. Ht. 60′–100′; diam. 2′–4½′. **Habitat:** Moist, wooded slopes and along streams.

Umbrella Magnolia, *Magnolia tripetala*
Field Marks: Leaves deciduous, crowded at the ends of branches, very large (up to 16″ long), tapering to the base, lower surface pale with fine hairs; flowers showy, up to 10″ across, with 9 or 12 petal-like parts, rather bad-smelling; fruits cone-like, pink or red at maturity, up to 8″ long, with pink or red seeds. Ht. 30′–50′; diam. 6″–18″. **Habitat:** Moist woods, along streams.

Southern Magnolia

Sweetbay

Cucumbertree

Umbrella Magnolia

MAGNOLIAS, YELLOW-POPLAR, PAWPAW, SASSAFRAS

Leaves alternate, simple, entire but sometimes lobed.

Bigleaf Magnolia, *Magnolia macrophylla*

Field Marks: Leaves deciduous, crowded at the ends of branches, up to 30″ long, up to 10″ wide, with silvery hairs on the lower surface, with ear-like lobes at the base; flowers creamy white, more or less cup-shaped, with 9 petal-like parts up to 8″ long, the inner 6 with a purple spot near the base. Ht. 30′–50′; diam. ½′–1½′. **Habitat:** Rich woods. **Comment:** Fraser magnolia, *M. fraseri*, lacks silver hairs on the leaves and has slightly smaller flowers.

Yellow-poplar, *Liriodendron tulipifera*

Field Marks: Leaves 4-lobed (rarely 6-lobed), broadest near the base, up to 5″ long, up to 6″ wide, not hairy; twigs with conspicuous circular scars; flowers tulip-shaped, yellow-green, with 6 green petals marked with orange at the base. Ht. 75′–175′; diam. 3′–7′. **Habitat:** Rich woods.

Pawpaw, *Asimina triloba*

Field Marks: Leaves broadest above the middle, tapering to the base, up to 12″ long, up to 6″ wide, thin, with few or no hairs at maturity; flowers maroon, with 6 leathery petals about 1″ long; fruits yellow, thick, and cylindrical, up to 4″ long. Ht. 15′–40′; diam. 4″–12″. **Habitat:** Rich woods, thickets.

Sassafras, *Sassafras albidum*

Field Marks: Leaves of three kinds—unlobed, 2-lobed mittens, and 3-lobed mittens, up to 6″ long, spicy-fragrant when crushed; twigs green. Ht. 20′–70′; diam. 6″–4′. **Habitat:** Open woods, thickets, fencerows.

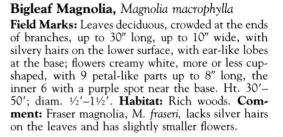

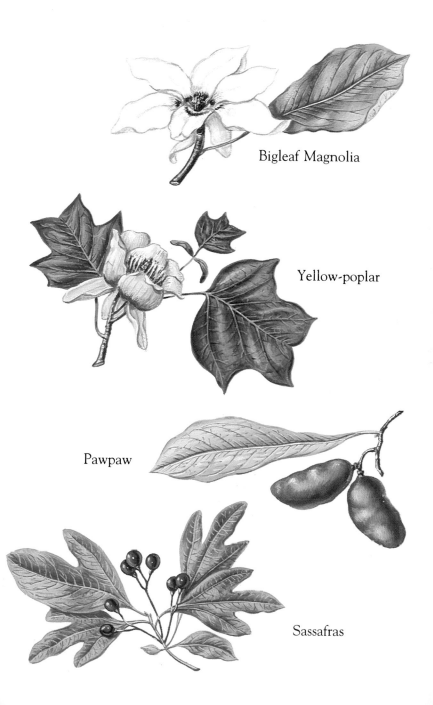

Bigleaf Magnolia

Yellow-poplar

Pawpaw

Sassafras

CALIFORNIA-LAUREL, REDBAY, SYCAMORES

Leaves alternate, simple.

California-laurel, *Umbellularia californica*

Field Marks: Leaves evergreen, leathery, lanceolate, without teeth, up to 5″ long, with a spicy odor when handled; fruits fleshy, yellow-green or purple-green at maturity, up to 1″ long, containing 1 seed. Ht. 20′–85′; diam. 1′–4′. **Habitat:** Rich woods, mountain slopes.

Redbay, *Persea borbonia*

Field Marks: Leaves evergreen, shiny, usually smooth or only sparsely hairy, lanceolate, without teeth, up to 8″ long, with a spicy odor when handled; twigs green, smooth; fruits fleshy, nearly spherical, dark blue, about ½″ in diameter. Ht. 20′–75′; diam. 1′–4′. **Habitat:** Wet ground. **Comment:** Swampbay, *P. palustris*, has hairy twigs and leaves.

American Sycamore, *Platanus occidentalis*

Field Marks: Leaves deciduous, coarsely toothed or shallowly lobed along the edges, hairy on the veins, up to 10″ long and as wide as they are long or wider, with large leaf-like structures (stipules) at the base of the leafstalks; bark peeling into long shreds, exposing the pale inner bark; fruits round and dry, up to 1½″ in diameter and dangling from a long stalk. Ht. 75′–120′; diam. 3′–12′. **Habitat:** Wet ground.

Arizona Sycamore, *Platanus wrightii*

Field Marks: Leaves deciduous, up to 10″ long and usually as wide, hairy on the lower surface, with 5 or 7 deeply cut lobes; bark peeling away, exposing the white inner bark; fruits borne several in a row, round and dry, up to 1″ in diameter. Ht. 25′–100′; diam. 3′–12′. **Habitat:** Along streams in deep canyons.

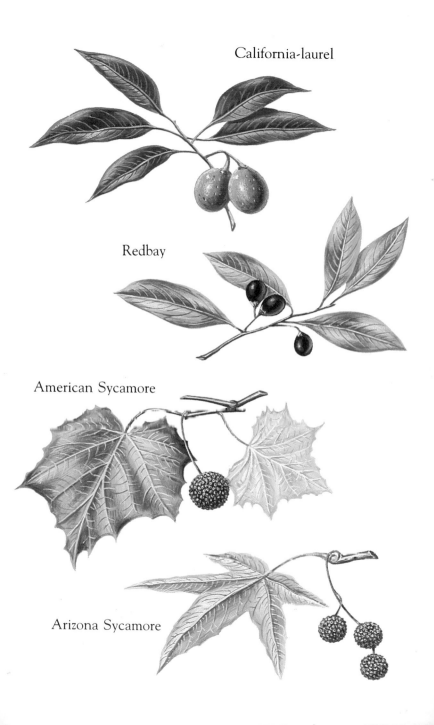

California-laurel

Redbay

American Sycamore

Arizona Sycamore

SWEETGUM, WITCH-HAZEL, ELMS

Leaves alternate, simple, toothed and/or lobed.

Sweetgum, *Liquidambar styraciflua*

Field Marks: Leaves star-shaped, 5-lobed or 7-lobed, toothed, usually smooth, up to 7″ long and about as wide; twigs sometimes with cork-like wings; fruits in the form of dry, spiny balls 1″–1½″ in diameter. Ht. 70′–140′; diam. 1½′–5′. **Habitat:** Bottomland woods.

Witch-hazel, *Hamamelis virginiana*

Field Marks: Leaves usually with scalloped edges, smooth except on the veins on the lower surface, 3″–6″ long; fruits woody, less than 1″ long, with a pair of beaks. Ht. 15′–30′; diam. 6″–12″. **Habitat:** Rich woods.

Siberian Elm, *Ulmus pumila*

Field Marks: Leaves smaller than most elm leaves, up to 3″ long, and with only single teeth along the edges; flowers appearing in the spring. Ht. 10′–30′; diam. 4″–14″. **Habitat:** This introduced species, usually found planted, sometimes seeds and spreads in cities or along country roads. **Comments:** This tree is often mistaken for the Chinese elm, *U. parvifolia,* a species that blooms during the autumn.

Winged Elm, *Ulmus alata*

Field Marks: Leaves up to 3″ long, only slightly asymmetrical at the base, with a double row of teeth along the edges; twigs usually with corky wings. Ht. 15′–70′; diam. 8″–3½′. **Habitat:** Dry soil, often on bluffs, less commonly in low, flat areas.

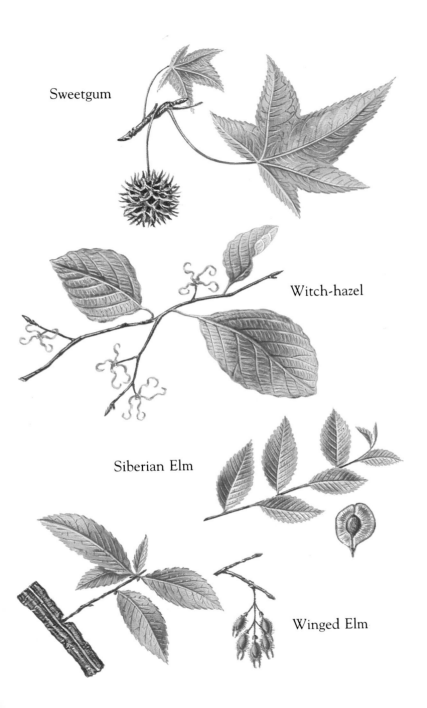

Sweetgum

Witch-hazel

Siberian Elm

Winged Elm

ELMS, WATER-ELM, HACKBERRY

Leaves alternate, simple, toothed.

American Elm, *Ulmus americana*
Field Marks: Leaves coarsely double-toothed, asymmetrical at the base, smooth to the touch on the upper surface, up to 6″ long, about half as wide; fruits flat, winged, with a notch at the tip, with hairy edges. Ht. 60′–120′; diam. 2½′–10′. **Habitat:** Bottomland woods, ravines, slopes.

Slippery Elm, *Ulmus rubra*
Field Marks: Leaves coarsely double-toothed, asymmetrical at the base, rough to the touch on the upper surface, up to 8″ long, about half as wide; fruits flat, winged, with smooth edges. Ht. 35′–100′; diam. 1′–2′. **Habitat:** Rich woods, bottomland woods.

Water-elm, *Planera aquatica*
Field Marks: Leaves single-toothed, asymmetrical at the base, slightly rough to the touch on the upper surface, 1½″–3½″ long, less than half as wide; fruits fleshy, not flat or winged. Ht. 10′–45′; diam. 6″–18″. **Habitat:** Swamps, bottomland woods.

Hackberry, *Celtis occidentalis*
Field Marks: Leaves usually coarsely toothed, often rough to the touch on the upper surface, asymmetrical at the base; bark covered with numerous warty projections; fruits fleshy, spherical, dark purple at maturity, at least ½″ in diameter. Ht. 30′–100′; diam. 10″–4½′. **Habitat:** Bottomland woods, along streams, less commonly in rocky woods.

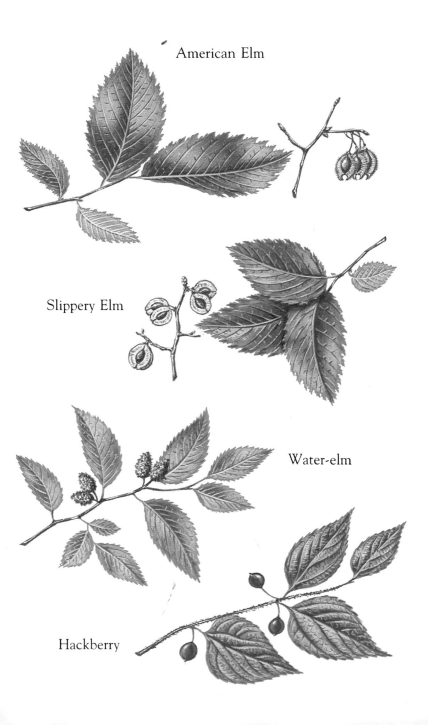

American Elm

Slippery Elm

Water-elm

Hackberry

HACKBERRIES, MULBERRIES, OSAGE-ORANGE

Leaves alternate, simple.

Sugarberry, *Celtis laevigata*

Field Marks: Leaves usually more than twice as long as broad, with few or no teeth, asymmetrical at base, usually smooth to the touch on the upper surface, 3"–6" long; trunk usually with warty projections; fruits fleshy, spherical, orange or yellow, less than ½" in diameter. Ht. 40'–90'; diam. 1'–4'. **Habitat:** Bottomland woods. **Comment:** Georgia hackberry, *C. tenuifolia,* is a low-growing tree of rocky soils with leaves usually less than 3" long.

Red Mulberry, *Morus rubra*

Field Marks: Leaves sometimes unlobed, 2-lobed, or 3-lobed, hairy, toothed, up to 8" long, containing milky sap; berries fleshy, red but turning dark at maturity. Ht. 15'–80'; diam. 10"–5'. **Habitat:** Bottomland forests. **Comment:** White mulberry, *M. alba,* introduced from Asia, has smooth leaves and usually paler fruits.

Osage-orange, *Maclura pomifera*

Field Marks: Leaves broadly lanceolate, heart-shaped at the base, smooth and without teeth, up to 6" long, about half as wide, containing a milky sap; twigs often with stout thorns; fruits hard but fleshy, spherical, yellow-green, up to 6" in diameter, containing milky sap. Ht. 15'–60'; diam. 8"–3½'. **Habitat:** Bottomland woods; often planted along fencerows.

Paper Mulberry, *Broussonetia papyrifera*

Field Marks: Leaves unlobed, 2-lobed, or 3-lobed, toothed, softly hairy, up to 8" long, containing milky sap; fruits orange or red, nearly 1" in diameter. Ht. 15'–50'; diam. 6"–2'. **Habitat:** An introduced species, this tree is now found along roads and around old homesites.

Sugarberry

Red Mulberry

Osage-orange

Paper Mulberry

BUTTERNUT, WALNUT, PECAN, HICKORIES

Leaves alternate, pinnately compound, with toothed leaflets.

Butternut, *Juglans cinerea*

Field Marks: Leaves with 11–19 leaflets; each leaflet lanceolate, usually sticky when young, 2″–4″ long, strongly scented when crushed; bark gray or light brown; fruits oblong, up to 3″ long, covered with short, dense, sticky hairs and containing a nut with a rich, buttery flavor. Ht. 40′–85′; diam. 1′–4′. **Habitat:** Rich woods.

Black Walnut, *Juglans nigra*

Field Marks: Leaves with 13–23 leaflets; each leaflet lanceolate, asymmetrical at the base, smooth or hairy but not sticky, up to 3½″ long, strongly scented when crushed; bark dark; fruits spherical, smooth and green at first, about 1½″ in diameter, containing a nut with a deeply grooved, woody shell. Ht. 50′–150′; diam. 1½′–6′. **Habitat:** Rich woods, bottomland forests.

Pecan, *Carya illinoensis*

Field Marks: Leaves with 9–15 leaflets; each leaflet lanceolate and curved, asymmetrical at the base, smooth or slightly hairy, 3″–8″ long, 1″–3″ wide; fruits oblong, hairy, 1½″–2″ long, containing a cylindrical nut with a thin shell and sweet kernel. Ht. 60′–180′; diam. 2′–8′. **Habitat:** Bottomland forests.

Water Hickory, *Carya aquatica*

Field Marks: Leaves with 7–13 leaflets; each leaflet lanceolate and usually curved, asymmetrical at the base, hairy, 2½″–4″ long, ½″–1½″ wide; fruits flattened, with 4 conspicuous wings and yellow scales, up to 1½″ long, containing a flattened nut with a thin shell and bitter kernel. Ht. 40′–110′; diam. 1′–4′. **Habitat:** Swamps, bottomland forests. **Comment:** Nutmeg hickory, *C. myristiciformis*, is similar but has round, thick-shelled nuts and leaves that are not curved.

Butternut

Black Walnut

Pecan

Water Hickory

HICKORIES

Leaves alternate, pinnately compound, with toothed leaflets.

Bitternut Hickory, *Carya cordiformis*

Field Marks: Leaves with 7–11 leaflets; each leaflet lanceolate, asymmetrical at the base, hairy on the lower surface, 4″–6″ long, about 1″ wide; buds elongated, mustard yellow; fruits nearly spherical, with yellow hairs, ¾″–1½″ in diameter, containing a spherical nut with a thin shell and bitter kernel. Ht. 40′–110′; diam. 1′–3½′. **Habitat:** Bottomland forests, wooded slopes.

Mockernut Hickory, *Carya tomentosa*

Field Marks: Leaves with 5–9 leaflets; each leaflet lanceolate but widest above the middle, densely hairy, 5″–9″ long, up to 5″ broad; buds large, hairy; fruits spherical, smooth or slightly hairy, 1½″–3½″ in diameter, with a thick husk, containing a rounded nut with a thick shell and sweet kernel. Ht. 45′–110′; diam. 1′–5′. **Habitat:** Wooded slopes.

Shagbark Hickory, *Carya ovata*

Field Marks: Leaves usually with 5 leaflets; each leaflet widest above the middle, hairy on the lower surface, 4″–7″ long, up to 3″ broad; buds large, hairy; bark peeling off in long strips; fruits usually spherical, smooth or sometimes slightly hairy, 1½″–2″ in diameter, containing a whitish nut with a thin shell and edible kernel. Ht. 50′–150′; diam. 1′–5′. **Habitat:** Rich woods, wooded slopes.

Shellbark Hickory, *Carya laciniosa*

Field Marks: Leaves usually with 7 leaflets; each leaflet widest above the middle, hairy on the lower surface, 6″–10″ long, up to 5″ broad; buds large, hairy; bark peeling off in long strips; fruits usually spherical, smooth or hairy, 2″-3″ in diameter, containing a whitish nut with a thick shell and sweet kernel. Ht. 60′–140′; diam. 1′–4′. **Habitat:** Bottomland forests, along rivers.

Bitternut Hickory

Mockernut Hickory

Shagbark Hickory

Shellbark Hickory

HICKORIES, BEECH, CHESTNUTS

Leaves alternate, pinnately compound or simple.

Pignut Hickory, *Carya glabra*

Field Marks: Leaves with 5 or 7 leaflets; each leaflet lanceolate, smooth on the lower surface, 3″–6″ long, up to 2″ wide; buds small, smooth; fruits pear-shaped, smooth, up to 2″ long, containing a nut with a thick shell and usually bitter kernel. Ht. 40′–125′; diam. 1′–4′. **Habitat:** Upland woods.

Black Hickory, *Carya texana*

Field Marks: Leaves with 5 or 7 leaflets; each leaflet lanceolate, with rusty hairs on the lower surface, 4″–6″ long, less than half as wide; buds small, covered with rusty and yellow hairs; fruits usually spherical, 1½″–2″ in diameter, covered with tiny yellow glands and containing a nut with a thick shell and sweet kernel. Ht. 30′–90′; diam. 10″–2′. **Habitat:** Dry, rocky woods. **Comment:** Sand hickory, C. *pallida*, has immature leaflets covered with silvery hairs.

American Beech, *Fagus grandifolia*

Field Marks: Leaves simple, lanceolate, tapering to a sharp point at the tip, sharply toothed, smooth or hairy on the lower surface, 3″–6″ long, 1½″–3″ broad; buds long, narrow, sharply pointed; bark smooth, gray; fruits in the form of small spiny burs containing 2 triangular nuts. Ht. 50′–100′; diam. 2′–12′. **Habitat:** Rich woods.

American Chestnut, *Castanea dentata*

Field Marks: Leaves simple, lanceolate, sharply toothed, usually smooth, 6″–10″ long, 1½″–3″ wide; fruits spherical, 2″–3″ in diameter, densely spiny, containing 1–3 nuts. Ht. 40′–110′; diam. 2′–4½′. **Habitat:** Wooded slopes. **Comment:** Allegheny chinkapin, C. *pumila*, is a small tree with woolly twigs and hairy leaves on the lower surface.

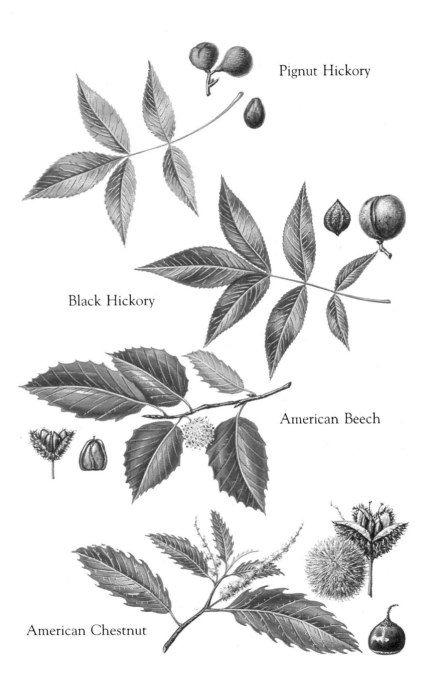

Pignut Hickory

Black Hickory

American Beech

American Chestnut

CHINKAPIN, TANOAK, OAKS

Leaves alternate, simple.

Golden Chinkapin, *Castanopsis chrysophylla*

Field Marks: Leaves evergreen, leathery, lanceolate, without teeth, covered with golden hairs on the lower surface, 3″–6″ long, up to 2″ wide; nuts slightly broader at the base, partially enclosed by a spiny bur 1″–1½″ in diameter. Ht. 40′–130′; diam. 1′–4′. **Habitat:** Rich woods, rocky woods, often in redwood forests.

Tanoak, *Lithocarpus densiflorus*

Field Marks: Leaves evergreen, leathery, broadly lanceolate, toothed, hairy on the lower surface, 3″–5″ long, more than half as wide; acorns up to 1″ long, ⅙ enclosed by a shallow cup with long, spreading scales. Ht. 30′–115′; diam. 1′–5′. **Habitat:** Mountain woods.

Bur Oak, *Quercus macrocarpa*

Field Marks: Leaves deciduous, leathery, with rounded lobes, including a pair of deep lobes between the middle and the base of the leaf, finely hairy on the lower surface, acorns 1″–3″ long, nearly as wide, ½–¾ enclosed by a cup with fringed scales along the edge. Ht. 50′–140′; diam. 2′–7′. **Habitat:** Bottom-land woods, less commonly on dry slopes.

Overcup Oak, *Quercus lyrata*

Field Marks: Leaves deciduous, not leathery, with 5–9 rather deep round lobes, pale and often hairy on the lower surface, 5″–10″ long, less than half as wide; acorns spherical or somewhat flattened, ⅔ to almost entirely enclosed by the cup. Ht. 50′–100′; diam. 1′–4′. **Habitat:** Bottomland woods, swamps.

Golden Chinkapin

Tanoak

Bur Oak

Overcup Oak

OAKS

Leaves deciduous, alternate, simple, usually round-lobed.

White Oak, *Quercus alba*
Field Marks: Leaves with 5–9 deep or shallow lobes, completely smooth on both surfaces, 5″–9″ long, 2″–4″ wide; acorns oblong, ¾″–1″ long, shiny, about ¼ enclosed by a cup with warty scales. Ht. 50′–150′; diam. 2′–5′. **Habitat:** Rich woods.

Post Oak, *Quercus stellata*
Field Marks: Leaves leathery, with 3 or 5 broad, squarish lobes, much broader above the middle, hairy or becoming smooth on the lower surface, 4″–8″ long, up to 4″ wide; acorns oblong, ½″–1″ long, ⅓–½ enclosed by the cup. Ht. 15′–65′; diam. 6″–3′. **Habitat:** Dry ridges, upland woods, bottomland woods. **Comment:** Durand oak, *Q. durandii*, has shallowly lobed or merely wavy-edged leaves and small acorns similar to those of post oak but ¼ enclosed by the cup.

Gambel Oak, *Quercus gambelii*
Field Marks: Leaves leathery, yellow-green, with 5–9 rather deep lobes, hairy on the lower surface, 3″–6″ long, 1½″–3″ wide; acorns spherical to oblong, ½″–¾″ long, ⅓–½ enclosed by a cup with hairy scales. Ht. 20′–65′; diam. 6″–5′. **Habitat:** Rocky canyons, dry wooded slopes.

California White Oak, *Quercus lobata*
Field Marks: Leaves with 9–11 rather deep lobes, hairy and with conspicuous yellow veins on the lower surface, 2½″–4″ long, 1″–2″ wide; acorns long and pointed, 1½″–2¼″ long, ⅕–¼ enclosed by a cup having scales with white hairs. Ht. 50′–100′; diam. 1½′–5′. **Habitat:** Wooded valleys and foothills. **Comment:** Blue oak, *Q. douglasii*, has acorns less than 1½″ long, about ⅕ covered by a warty cup.

White Oak

Post Oak

Gambel Oak

California White Oak

OAKS

Leaves deciduous, alternate, simple, with coarse or jagged teeth.

Swamp White Oak, *Quercus bicolor*

Field Marks: Leaves with many coarse, rounded teeth, the lower surface conspicuously paler and usually hairy, widest just above the middle, 5″–10″ long, nearly half as wide; acorns oblong, about 1″ long, ¼–⅓ enclosed by the cup, borne on a stalk up to 4″ long. Ht. 40′–105′; diam. 1′–7′. **Habitat:** Swamps, bottomland forests.

Swamp Chestnut Oak, *Quercus michauxii*

Field Marks: Leaves with many coarse, rounded teeth, softly hairy on the lower surface, widest near the middle, 4″–8″ long, about half as wide; acorns spherical to oblong, 1″–1½″ long, ¼–⅓ enclosed by the cup. Ht. 50′–120′; diam. 2′–6′. **Habitat:** Swamps, bottomland forests.

Chestnut Oak, *Quercus prinus*

Field Marks: Leaves coarsely round-toothed, finely hairy on the lower surface, widest near the middle, 5″–9″ long, about half as wide; acorns oblong, brown and shiny, 1″–1½″ long, ½ enclosed by the slightly hairy cup. Ht. 40′–100′; diam. 1½′–4′. **Habitat:** Rocky ridges, wooded slopes.

Chinkapin Oak, *Quercus muhlenbergii*

Field Marks: Leaves usually with strongly jagged teeth, finely hairy on the lower surface, 4″–8″ long, 1½″–5″ wide; acorn oblong, light brown and shiny, up to 1″ long, ½ enclosed by the hairy cup. Ht. 50′–120′; diam. 1½′–5′. **Habitat:** Wooded slopes, rocky ridges.

Swamp White Oak

Swamp Chestnut Oak

Chestnut Oak

Chinkapin Oak

OAKS

Leaves alternate, simple.

Live Oak, *Quercus virginiana*

Field Marks: Leaves evergreen, leathery, widest at about the middle or slightly above, without teeth, with pale hairs on the lower surface, 2½"–5" long, up to 2½" wide; acorns longer than wide, up to ½" long, ⅓ enclosed by the hairy cup. Ht. 40'–60'; diam. 2'–8'. **Habitat:** Rich woods, sandy barrens.

Arizona White Oak, *Quercus arizonica*

Field Marks: Leaves often evergreen, leathery, sometimes with wavy teeth along the edges, widest near middle, hairy on the lower surface, 2"–4" long, up to half as wide; acorns oblong, shiny, brown, about ½" long, ⅓–½ enclosed by the cup. Ht. 15'–60'; diam. 6"–3½'. **Habitat:** Rocky woods, mountain slopes. **Comments:** Netleaf oak, *Q. reticulata,* usually has jagged-toothed leaves that often are gray-green on the upper surface. Toumey oak, *Q. toumeyi,* has blue-green evergreen leaves with a few small teeth. Gray oak, *Q. grisea,* has gray-green, leathery evergreen leaves without teeth.

Emory Oak, *Quercus emoryi*

Field Marks: Leaves often evergreen, widest near base, usually with a few sharp teeth, sparsely hairy on the lower surface; acorns narrowly elongated, ½"–¾" long, ⅓–½ enclosed by the cup. Ht. 15'–50'; diam. 6"–3½'. **Habitat:** Rocky woodlands and foothills.

Northern Red Oak, *Quercus rubra*

Field Marks: Leaves deciduous, with 7–9 shallow to moderately deep, bristle-tipped lobes, hairy on the lower surface only where the veins come together, 5"–9" long, 2½"–5" wide; acorns oval, ¾"–1¼" long, ¼ or less enclosed by the cup. Ht. 40'–100'; diam. 1'–4½'. **Habitat:** Rich woods, upland forests.

Live Oak

Arizona White Oak

Emory Oak

Northern Red Oak

OAKS

Leaves alternate, simple, deciduous, with bristle-tipped lobes.

Pin Oak, *Quercus palustris*

Field Marks: Leaves with 5–7 deep lobes, smooth except for hairs where the veins come together on the lower surface, 4″–6″ long, up to 4″ wide; lower branches hanging toward the ground; acorns spherical, about ½″ in diameter, ¼ enclosed by the cup. Ht. 40′–80′; diam. 10″–3′. **Habitat:** Wet ground. **Comments:** Northern pin oak, *Q. ellipsoidalis*, has similar leaves but elongated acorns ¾″ in diameter and nearly ½ enclosed by the cup. Bear oak, *Q. ilicifolia*, has shallower lobes and spherical acorns ⅓–½ enclosed by the cup.

Southern Red Oak, *Quercus falcata*

Field Marks: Leaves with 3–7 deep lobes with the terminal lobe curved, hairy on the lower surface, 6″–10″ long, 4″–6″ wide; acorns spherical, about ½″ in diameter, ⅓ enclosed by the cup. Ht. 50′–100′; diam. 1½′–5′. **Habitat:** Upland forests.

Cherrybark Oak, *Quercus pagoda*

Field Marks: Leaves with 5 or 7 deep lobes with the terminal lobe not curved, hairy on the lower surface, 5″–10″ long, 4″–6″ wide; acorns spherical, ½″–¾″ in diameter, nearly ½ enclosed by cup. Ht. 60′–100′; diam. 1½′–5′. **Habitat:** Bottomland woods.

Turkey Oak, *Quercus laevis*

Field Marks: Leaves with 3 or 5 deep lobes, the terminal lobe curved, yellow-green, smooth on the lower surface; acorns spherical, 1″–1¼″ in diameter, ⅓ enclosed by the cup. Ht. 20′–50′; diam. 10″–2′. **Habitat:** Dry, often sandy soil.

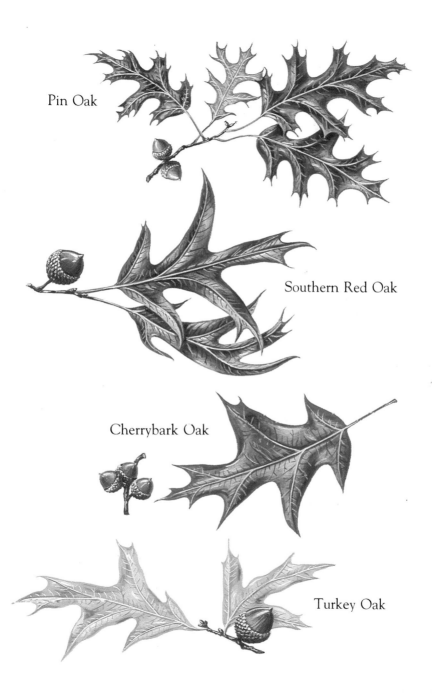

Pin Oak

Southern Red Oak

Cherrybark Oak

Turkey Oak

OAKS

Leaves alternate, simple, deciduous, with bristle-tipped lobes.

Black Oak, *Quercus velutina*

Field Marks: Leaves with 5–7 deep lobes, usually smooth on the lower surface except for hairs where the veins come together, 5″–11″ long, 3″–5½″ wide; buds gray, hairy, with sharp ridges; acorns spherical to oblong, ½″–¾″ long, ⅓–½ enclosed by the cup, which has spreading scales at the edge. Ht. 50′–90′; diam. 1′–4′. **Habitat:** Upland woods.

Shumard Oak, *Quercus shumardii*

Field Marks: Leaves with 5–9 very deep lobes, dark green and shiny, smooth on the lower surface except where the veins come together, 4″–8″ long, 3″–5″ wide; acorns oblong, ½″–1″ long, ⅓ enclosed by the cup. Ht. 40′–125′; diam. 1′–6′. **Habitat:** Rich bottomland forests.

Scarlet Oak, *Quercus coccinea*

Field Marks: Leaves with 5–9 deep lobes, bright green and shiny, smooth on the lower surface except where the veins come together, 4″–6″ long, up to 4″ wide; acorns egg-shaped, ¾″–1″ long, ⅓–½ enclosed by the cup. Ht. 60′–100′; diam. 1′–3′. **Habitat:** Upland woods.

Water Oak, *Quercus nigra*

Field Marks: Leaves with 3 or 5 very shallow lobes or even unlobed, smooth on the lower surface except where the veins come together, 2″–4″ long, up to half as wide; acorns spherical, about ½″ in diameter, ¼–⅓ enclosed by the cup. Ht. 25′–80′; diam. 10″–3½′. **Habitat:** Bottomland woods. **Comment:** Arkansas oak, *Q. arkansana*, has 3 very shallow lobes toward the upper part of the leaf and acorns less than ½″ in diameter.

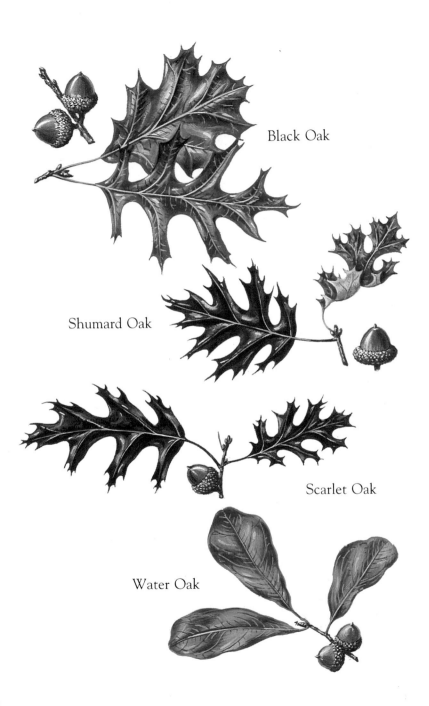

Black Oak

Shumard Oak

Scarlet Oak

Water Oak

OAKS

Leaves alternate, simple, often without teeth or lobes.

Blackjack Oak, *Quercus marilandica*

Field Marks: Leaves deciduous, leathery, with 3 broad shallow lobes near the upper end, hairy on the lower surface, 3″–8″ long, often nearly as wide; acorns spherical, ¾″–1″ in diameter, ½ enclosed by the cup. Ht. 15′–50′; diam. 6″–2′. **Habitat:** Dry soil.

Laurel Oak, *Quercus laurifolia*

Field Marks: Leaves nearly evergreen, leathery, usually without lobes or teeth, dark green and shiny, 2″–4″ long, up to 1″ wide; acorns a little longer than they are wide, nearly 1″ long, ¼ enclosed by the cup. Ht. 50′–100′; diam. 1′–4′. **Habitat:** Low woods, swamps. **Comment:** Myrtle oak, *Q. myrtifolia*, has evergreen leaves up to 2″ long and acorns only ½″ long.

Willow Oak, *Quercus phellos*

Field Marks: Leaves deciduous, without teeth, resembling willow leaves, 2½″–5″ long, up to 1″ wide; acorns spherical, about ½″ in diameter, ¼ enclosed by the cup. Ht. 50′–100′; diam. 1′–4′. **Habitat:** Bottomland woods, swamps, sandy uplands.

Shingle Oak, *Quercus imbricaria*

Field Marks: Leaves deciduous, without teeth, hairy on the lower surface, 4″–6″ long, 1″–2½″ wide; acorns spherical, about ½″ in diameter, ⅓ enclosed by the cup. Ht. 40′–100′; diam. 1′–4′. **Habitat:** Bottomland forests, upland woods.

Blackjack Oak

Laurel Oak

Willow Oak

Shingle Oak

OAKS, HORNBEAMS, BIRCH

Leaves alternate, simple, usually toothed.

Interior Live Oak, *Quercus wislizenii*

Field Marks: Leaves evergreen, toothed or without teeth, smooth on the lower surface, 1″–1½″ long, less than 1″ wide; acorns about 1″ long, ½–⅔ enclosed by the cup. Ht. 15′–50′; diam. 2′–6′. **Habitat:** Dry mountain slopes. **Comments:** Coast live oak, *Q. agrifolia*, has usually deciduous, leathery, toothed leaves up to 4″ long and slender, pointed acorns up to 1½″ long. Canyon live oak, *Q. chrysolepis*, has evergreen, leathery, usually toothed leaves and acorns rounded at the tip.

Eastern Hophornbeam, *Ostrya virginiana*

Field Marks: Leaves deciduous, narrowly ovate, toothed along the edges, smooth on the lower surface except where the veins come together, 2″–5″ long, up to 2″ wide; bark broken up into narrow strips; fruits are groups of small air-filled bladders. Ht. 15′–60′; diam. 6″–2′. **Habitat:** Moist slopes, upland woods.

American Hornbeam, *Carpinus caroliniana*

Field Marks: Leaves deciduous, narrowly ovate, toothed along the edges, smooth on the lower surface except where the veins come together, 2″–5″ long, up to 2″ wide; bark smooth; fruits in the form of groups of leafy 3-lobed structures with a small nut at the base. Ht. 15′–40′; diam. 6″–2′. **Habitat:** Bottomland woods, along streams.

Sweet Birch, *Betula lenta*

Field Marks: Leaves deciduous, ovate, toothed, hairy on the veins on the lower surface, 2½″–5″ long, 1½″–3″ wide; "cones" about 1″ long, ½″ wide, upright. Ht. 20′–75′; diam. 10″–4½′. **Habitat:** Rich woods, often in the mountains.

Interior Live Oak

Eastern Hophornbeam

American Hornbeam

Sweet Birch

BIRCHES

Leaves alternate, simple, toothed, deciduous.

Yellow Birch, *Betula alleghaniensis*
Field Marks: Leaves ovate, hairy on the veins on the lower surface, 2″–5″ long, up to 2″ wide; bark silvery gray at first, eventually peeling off into ragged strips, becoming yellow-brown; "cones" 1″–1½″ long, ½″–⅔″ wide, upright. Ht. 35′–80′; diam. 10″–4′.
Habitat: Rich upland woods.

River Birch, *Betula nigra*
Field Marks: Leaves ovate or triangularly ovate, hairy on the veins on the lower surface, 2″–4″ long, 1″–2½″ wide; bark eventually breaking and separating into papery, curled, red-brown scales; "cones" 1″–1½″ long, ½″–⅔″ wide, usually hanging from the branchlets. Ht. 45′–90′; diam. 1′–5′. **Habitat:** Along streams, bottomland forests.

Paper Birch, *Betula papyrifera*
Field Marks: Leaves ovate to triangularly ovate, smooth or softly hairy on the lower surface, 2″–4″ long, 1″–2″ wide; bark smooth and ivory white at first, becoming black-blotched, eventually breaking and rolling back into large papery sheets; "cones" 1″–1½″ long, hanging from the branchlets. Ht. 45′–80′; diam. 1′–4′. **Habitat:** Rich wooded slopes, along streams, around lakes.

Gray Birch, *Betula populifolia*
Field Marks: Leaves triangularly ovate, narrowed to an elongated and pointed tip, smooth on the lower surface, 2″–3½″ long, 1″–2″ wide; bark creamy white with dark triangular mottling; "cones" cylindrical, ¾″ long, hanging from the branchlets. Ht. 10′–40′; diam. 4″–18″. **Habitat:** Sandy open soil.
Comment: Blue birch, *B. caerulea-grandis*, has pink-white bark and drooping "cones" 1″–2″ long.

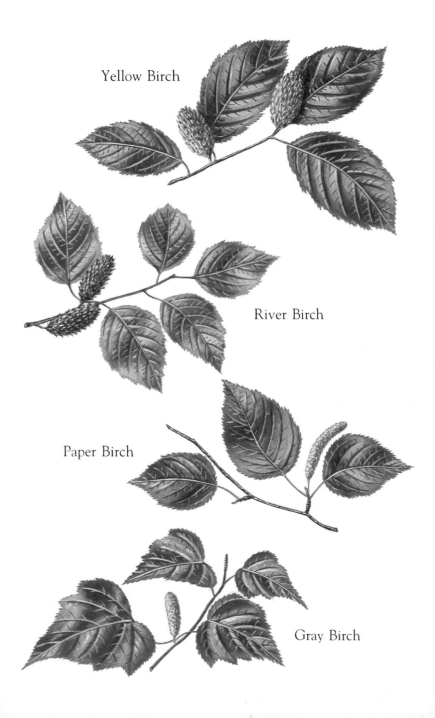

Yellow Birch

River Birch

Paper Birch

Gray Birch

ALDERS, HORSETAIL CASUARINA, LOBLOLLY-BAY, BASSWOODS

Leaves alternate, simple, toothed or reduced to scales.

Red Alder, *Alnus rubra*

Field Marks: Leaves deciduous, more or less leathery, coarsely toothed, with rust-colored hairs on the lower surface, 3″–5″ long, 1½″–3″ wide; bark blue-gray and white; "cones" woody, upright, about 1″ long and ½″ wide. Ht. 70′–130′; diam. 1½′–2½′. **Habitat:** Rich bottomlands, along streams. **Comments:** White alder, A. *rhombifolia*, has finely toothed, yellow-green leaves and "cones" up to ½″ long. Sitka alder, A. *sinuata*, is a smaller tree with coarsely toothed leaves 3″–6″ long, and short, thick "cones." Mountain alder, A. *tenuifolia*, is a small tree with coarsely toothed leaves 2″–3″ long.

Horsetail Casuarina, *Casuarina equisetifolia*

Field Marks: Leaves reduced to minute scales about ¹⁄₁₀″ long, borne along simple, drooping, jointed branchlets reminiscent of horsetail stems; "cones" woody, spherical, ½″–⅔″ in diameter. Ht. 50′–100′; diam. 10″–2′. **Habitat:** Introduced from Australia, this unusual-looking tree is extensively planted in warm regions of North America, particularly southern Florida.

Loblolly-bay, *Gordonia lasianthus*

Field Marks: Leaves evergreen, leathery, oblong, with many minute teeth along the edges, smooth, 3″–6″ long, up to 2″ wide; flowers white, fragrant, 2½″–3½″ across, with 5 petals. Ht. 30′–75′; diam. 6″–20″. **Habitat:** Swamps, wet ground. **Comments:** Virginia stewartia, *Stewartia malacodendron*, and mountain stewartia, S. *ovata*, are similar in having large white 5-petaled flowers, but they have thin, deciduous leaves.

American Basswood, *Tilia americana*

Field Marks: Leaves deciduous, oval, heart-shaped at the base, coarsely toothed, smooth or hairy on the lower surface where the veins come together, 5″–10″ long, often nearly as wide; fruits hard, spherical, up to ½″ in diameter, attached by a slender stalk to a paddle-like leaf. Ht. 50′–120′; diam. 1′–5′. **Habitat:** Rich bottomland woods, wooded slopes. **Comment:** White basswood, T. *heterophylla*, has white hairs completely covering the lower surface of the leaves.

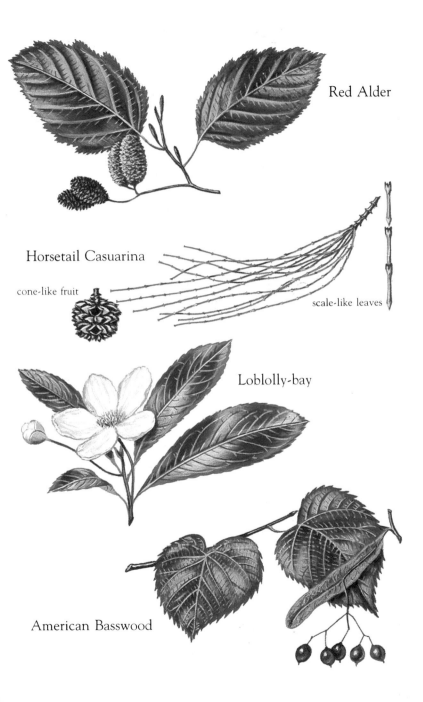

Red Alder

Horsetail Casuarina

cone-like fruit

scale-like leaves

Loblolly-bay

American Basswood

TAMARISK, POPLARS

Leaves alternate, simple, deciduous.

French Tamarisk, *Tamarix gallica*

Field Marks: Leaves scale-like, pale green, about ⅕″ long; flowers tiny, pink, with 5 petals, crowded into narrow terminal sprays. Ht. 10′–30′; diam. 2″–6″. **Habitat:** Along dry, sandy banks of creeks. **Comments:** Native of southern Europe but introduced into North America for erosion control. It is now widespread, particularly in the southern and southwestern United States.

Swamp Cottonwood, *Populus heterophylla*

Field Marks: Leaves broadly ovate, heart-shaped at the base, toothed, with white hairs on the lower surface, particularly when young; leaf stalks not flattened; fruits in the form of elongated clusters of ½″-long capsules. Ht. 50′–100′; diam. 1′–3′. **Habitat:** Swamps, bottomland woods.

Balsam Poplar, *Populus balsamifera*

Field Marks: Leaves ovate, not heart-shaped at the base, toothed, often with resinous dots on the lower surface; leaf stalks not flattened; buds gummy; fruits in the form of elongated clusters of ⅓″-long capsules. Ht. 50′–100′; diam. 1½′–6′. **Habitat:** Bottomlands, swamps.

Black Cottonwood, *Populus trichocarpa*

Field Marks: Leaves broadly ovate, rounded at the base, toothed, with rust-colored dots on the lower surface, 3″–4″ long, up to 2½″ wide; leaf stalks not flattened; buds gummy; fruits in the form of elongated clusters of ¼″-long capsules. Ht. 75′–150′; diam. 2½′–5′. **Habitat:** Wooded valleys, wet soil.

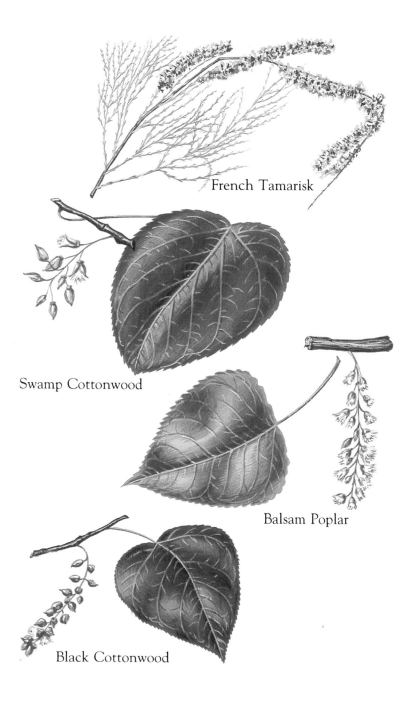

French Tamarisk

Swamp Cottonwood

Balsam Poplar

Black Cottonwood

POPLARS

Leaves alternate, simple, toothed, deciduous.

White Poplar, *Populus alba*
Field Marks: Leaves ovate, with a few large teeth, coated with a white felt on the lower surface, 2″–4″ long, up to 2″ wide; fruits in the form of elongated clusters of ¼″-long capsules. Ht. 30′–70′; diam. 10″–3′. **Habitat:** This native of Europe has been introduced into North America, where it can be found planted as an ornamental.

Narrowleaf Cottonwood, *Populus angustifolia*
Field Marks: Leaves lanceolate, mostly finely toothed, smooth, 2″–3½″ long, ½″–1¼″ wide; leaf stalks flattened near the base; buds gummy; fruits in the form of elongated clusters of ¼″-long capsules. Ht. 30′–70′; diam. 6″–18″. **Habitat:** Moist soil.

Eastern Cottonwood, *Populus deltoides*
Field Marks: Leaves triangularly ovate, coarsely toothed, smooth, 3″–7″ long, 4″–4½″ wide; leaf stalks strongly flattened; buds gummy; fruits in the form of elongated clusters of ⅓″-long capsules. Ht. 75′–150′; diam. 2′–6′. **Habitat:** Along rivers and streams, bottomland woods.

Fremont Cottonwood, *Populus fremontii*
Field Marks: Leaves triangularly ovate, coarsely toothed, usually smooth at maturity, 2½″–3″ long and about as wide; leaf stalks flattened; fruits in the form of elongated clusters of ⅓″-long capsules. Ht. 60′–100′; diam. 1′–5′. **Habitat:** Along streams, wet ground.

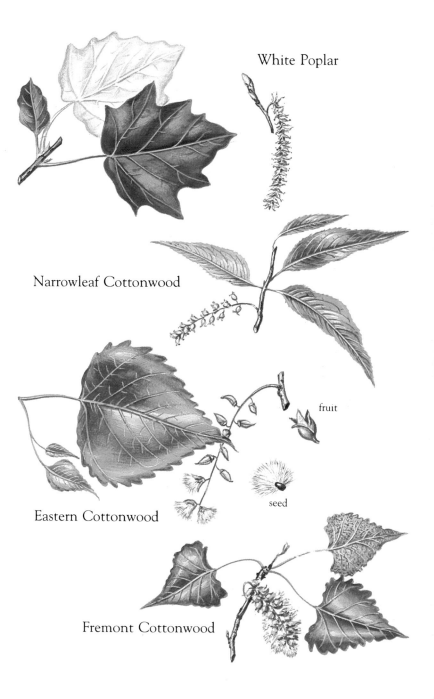

White Poplar

Narrowleaf Cottonwood

Eastern Cottonwood

fruit

seed

Fremont Cottonwood

ASPENS, WILLOWS

Leaves alternate, simple, toothed, deciduous.

Quaking Aspen, *Populus tremuloides*

Field Marks: Leaves very broadly ovate to almost spherical, finely toothed, smooth, 1"–3" long, nearly as broad; leaf stalks flattened near the base; buds slightly gummy; fruits in the form of elongated clusters of capsules, each less than ⅓" long. Ht. 35'–90'; diam. 6"–30". **Habitat:** A variety of habitats.

Bigtooth Aspen, *Populus grandidentata*

Field Marks: Leaves broadly ovate, with several large teeth, finely hairy, 2"–3" long and nearly as wide; leaf stalks flattened near the base; buds slightly gummy; fruits in the form of elongated clusters of capsules, each less than ⅓" long. Ht. 35'–75'; diam. 6"–30". **Habitat:** Along streams and lakes.

Peachleaf Willow, *Salix amygdaloides*

Field Marks: Leaves lanceolate, finely toothed, smooth but paler on the lower surface, 3"–6" long, ¾"–1¼" wide; fruits in the form of elongated clusters of capsules, each about ⅓" long. Ht. 20'–60'; diam. 6"–24". **Habitat:** Wet soil.

Black Willow, *Salix nigra*

Field Marks: Leaves narrowly lanceolate, finely toothed, smooth, green on both sides, 3"–6" long, ½"–¾" wide; fruits in the form of elongated clusters of capsules, each about ⅓" long. Ht. 30'–120'; diam. 1'–6'. **Habitat:** Wet ground. **Comment:** Silky willow, *S. sericea*, has silvery, silky hairs on the lower surface of the leaves.

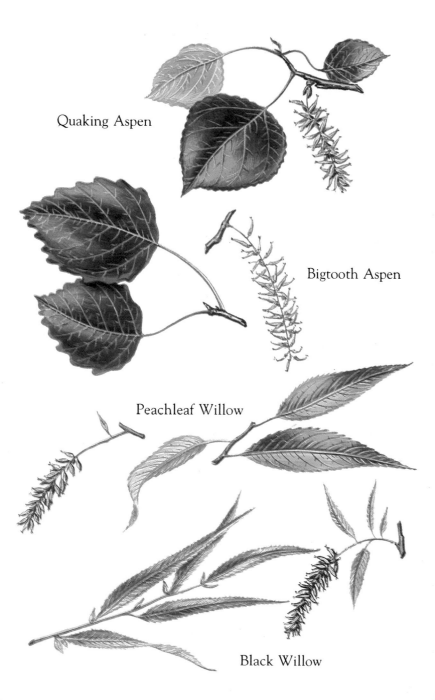

Quaking Aspen

Bigtooth Aspen

Peachleaf Willow

Black Willow

WILLOWS

Leaves alternate, simple, usually toothed, deciduous.

Crack Willow, *Salix fragilis*

Field Marks: Leaves lanceolate, finely toothed, smooth, paler on the lower surface, 3″–6″ long, ½″–1″ wide; branches brittle; fruits in the form of elongated clusters of capsules, each about ⅕″ long. Ht. 30′–100′; diam. 6″–30″. **Habitat:** Damp soil. **Comment:** Like the crack willow, the weeping willow, *S. babylonica*, with its pendulous branches, was introduced into the United States.

White Willow, *Salix alba*

Field Marks: Leaves lanceolate, finely toothed, smooth or hairy, 2″–4″ long, ½″–¾″ wide; fruits in the form of elongated clusters of capsules, each about ⅕″ long. Ht. 20′–75′; diam. 4″–24″. **Habitat:** Damp soil. **Comment:** This and basket willow, *S. viminalis*, which has narrower leaves with few or no teeth, are native to Europe.

Scouler Willow, *Salix scoulerana*

Field Marks: Leaves narrow, widest above the middle, wavy-edged, hairy on the lower surface, 2″–5″ long, ½″–1½″ wide; fruits in the form of clusters of densely hairy capsules, each about ⅓″ long. Ht. 10′–50′; diam. 4″–18″. **Habitat:** In wetlands, along roads. **Comments:** Other willows found in most states from the Rocky Mountains westward are Geyer willow, *S. geyerana*, with silvery leaves; arroyo willow, *S. lasiolepis*, with green, elliptic leaves broadest near the middle; and Pacific willow, *S. lasiandra*, with green, lanceolate leaves widest near the base.

Sandbar Willow (Coyote Willow), *Salix exigua*

Field Marks: Leaves very long and narrow, with few widely spaced teeth, smooth or hairy, 3″–6″ long, about ⅓″ wide; fruits in the form of elongated clusters of capsules, each about ⅓″ long. Ht. 10′–25′; diam. 3″–10″. **Habitat:** Sandbars along rivers and streams. **Comment:** Formerly classified as two distinct species, this tree is still known as the sandbar willow in the eastern part of its range and as the coyote willow in the West.

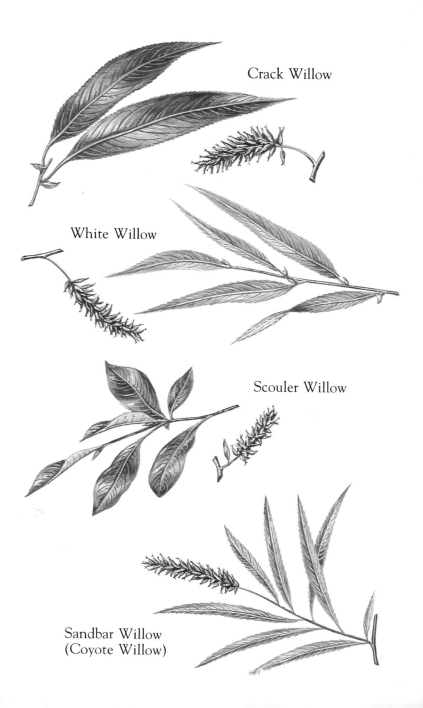

Crack Willow

White Willow

Scouler Willow

Sandbar Willow
(Coyote Willow)

SOURWOOD, MOUNTAIN-LAUREL, MADRONES

Leaves alternate, simple.

Sourwood, *Oxydendrum arboreum*

Field Marks: Leaves broadest near the middle, tapering to both ends, finely toothed, smooth, 4″–7″ long, 1″–3″ wide; fruits in the form of elongated, hanging clusters of capsules, each up to ½″ long. Ht. 25′–60′; diam. 10″–24″. **Habitat:** Woods, often in mountains.

Mountain-laurel, *Kalmia latifolia*

Field Marks: Leaves evergreen, broadest near the middle, without teeth, usually smooth, 2½″–4″ long, 1″–1½″ wide; flowers nearly 1″ across, with 5 white or pink petals lined with rose markings. Ht. 10′–30′; diam. 6″–20″. **Habitat:** Mountain woods, thickets, bogs.

Pacific Madrone, *Arbutus menziesii*

Field Marks: Leaves evergreen, leathery, widest near the middle, paler on the lower surface, 3″–5″ long, 1½″–3″ wide; fruits bright orange-red, spherical, about ½″ in diameter. Ht. 20′–120′; diam. 6″–48″. **Habitat:** Along streams, in woods, particularly in the mountains.

Arizona Madrone, *Arbutus arizonica*

Field Marks: Leaves evergreen, lanceolate, smooth, 1½″–3″ long, ½″–1″ wide; fruits orange-red, spherical, less than ½″ in diameter. Ht. 15′–50′; diam. 6″–18″. **Habitat:** Dry woodlands.

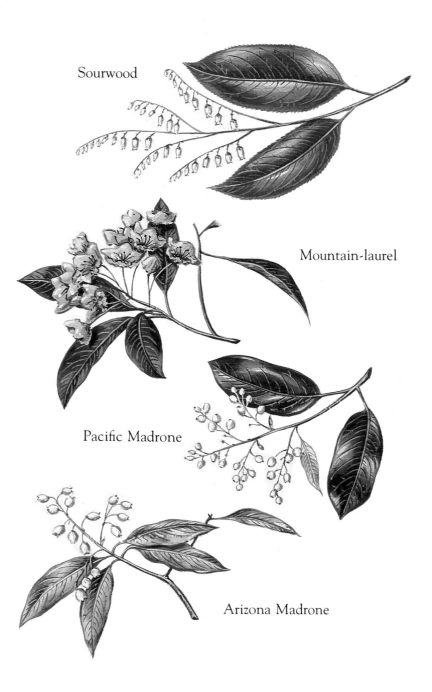

Sourwood

Mountain-laurel

Pacific Madrone

Arizona Madrone

BUMELIAS, PERSIMMON, SILVERBELLS, SWEETLEAF

Leaves alternate, simple, deciduous.

Gum Bumelia, *Bumelia lanuginosa*

Field Marks: Leaves widest near or above the middle, rounded at the tip, without teeth, densely hairy on the lower surface, 1"–2½" long, ¼"–¾" wide; branchlets with short, stout spines; fruits black, spherical, fleshy, about ½" in diameter. Ht. 15'–45'; diam. 6"–24". **Habitat:** Dry, often rocky soil. **Comment:** Buckthorn bumelia, *B. lycioides*, has sparsely hairy leaves.

Persimmon, *Diospyros virginiana*

Field Marks: Leaves widest near the middle, abruptly pointed at the tip, without teeth, paler and sometimes hairy on the lower surface, 3"–7" long, 1½"–3½" wide; fruits fleshy, orange, spherical, about ¾" in diameter. Ht. 25'–75'; diam. 6"–36". **Habitat:** Moist or dry woods, in fields.

Carolina Silverbell, *Halesia carolina*

Field Marks: Leaves widest near the middle, tapering to each end, pointed at the tip, finely toothed, smooth or hairy, 3"–6" long, 1½"–3½" wide; flowers white, bell-shaped, with petals ½"–1" long; fruits with 4 wings, 1½"–2" long. Ht. 25'–100'; diam. 6"–36". **Habitat:** Woods, often in mountains. **Comments:** Little silverbell, *H. parviflora*, has petals up to ½" long; two-winged silverbell, *H. diptera*, has 2-winged fruits.

Sweetleaf, *Symplocos tinctoria*

Field Marks: Leaves widest near the middle, tapering to either end, usually finely toothed, hairy and paler on the lower surface, 3"–6" long, ¾"–1½" wide; fruits fleshy, orange or brown, longer than wide, about ½" long. Ht. 10'–40'; diam. 6"–15". **Habitat:** Rich woods.

Gum Bumelia

Persimmon

Carolina Silverbell

Sweetleaf

CHERRIES

Leaves alternate, simple, usually toothed.

Chokecherry, *Prunus virginiana*

Field Marks: Leaves deciduous, usually widest near the middle, pointed at the tip, finely toothed, smooth, 2″–4″ long, ½″–1″ wide; leaf stalks with a pair of tiny swellings; flowers white, in elongated clusters; fruits fleshy, spherical, usually red or black, less than ½″ in diameter. Ht. 15′–30′; diam. 4″–10″. **Habitat:** Moist soil.

Black Cherry, *Prunus serotina*

Field Marks: Leaves deciduous, usually widest below the middle, pointed at the tip, finely toothed, smooth, 2½″–5″ long, 1″–1½″ wide; leaf stalks often with 1 or 2 tiny swellings; flowers white, in elongated clusters; fruits fleshy, spherical, black, less than ½″ in diameter. Ht. 35′–100′; diam. 10″–4′. **Habitat:** A variety of woods.

Carolina Laurelcherry, *Prunus caroliniana*

Field Marks: Leaves evergreen, widest near the middle, pointed at the tip, with or without a few teeth, smooth but paler on the lower surface, 2″–4½″ long, ½″–1½″ wide; flowers cream white, in elongated clusters; fruits fleshy, black, shiny, about ½″ long, slightly longer than wide. Ht. 15′–40′; diam. 6″–15″. **Habitat:** Rich woods.

Pin Cherry, *Prunus pensylvanica*

Field Marks: Leaves deciduous, lanceolate, pointed at the tip, finely toothed, smooth and paler on the lower surface, 3″–6″ long, ¾″–1¼″ wide; leaf stalks with a few swellings; flowers cream white, in short clusters; fruits fleshy, spherical, bright red, about ⅓″ in diameter. Ht. 20′–40′; diam. 8″–20″. **Habitat:** Woods and along streams.

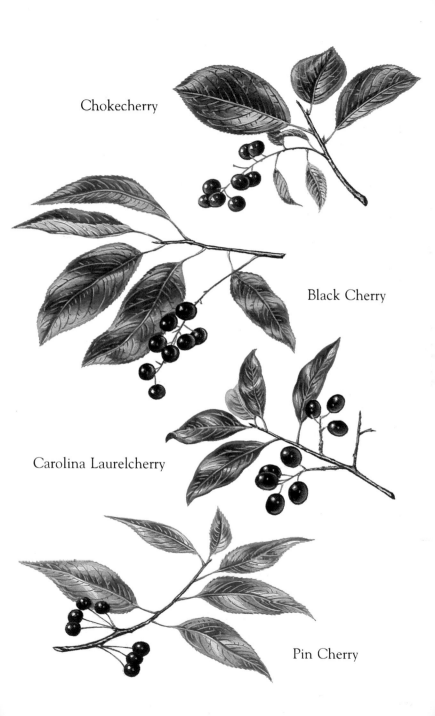

Chokecherry

Black Cherry

Carolina Laurelcherry

Pin Cherry

PLUMS, MOUNTAIN-ASHES, SERVICEBERRIES, CRAB APPLE

Leaves alternate, deciduous.

American Plum, *Prunus americana*

Field Marks: Young branches usually with spines; leaves simple, widest at the middle, toothed, hairy, 2″–4″ long, 1½″–2″ wide; leaf stalks usually with 2 conspicuous swellings; flowers 2–5 in a cluster, with 5 white petals; fruits fleshy, spherical, orange to red, sweet, ¾″–1″ in diameter. Ht. 8′–35′; diam. 4″–12″. **Habitat:** Woods and thickets. **Comment:** Canada plum, *P. nigra*, has thicker leaves with somewhat larger teeth and larger, sour fruits 1″–1¼″ in diameter.

American Mountain-ash, *Sorbus americana*

Field Marks: Leaves pinnately compound with 9–19 lanceolate, finely toothed, smooth or hairy, green leaflets; each leaflet 1″–3″ long; flowers numerous, tiny, white, massed together into large, broad, flat-topped clusters; fruits fleshy, orange-red, shiny, spherical, about ¼″ in diameter. Ht. 10′–35′; diam. 6″–22″. **Habitat:** Moist, rocky areas, often in the mountains. **Comment:** Showy mountain-ash, *S. decora*, has bluish or gray-green leaflets and slightly larger fruits.

Downy Serviceberry, *Amelanchier arborea*

Field Marks: Leaves simple, widest near the middle, rounded or slightly heart-shaped at the base, finely toothed, paler and hairy on the lower surface, 2″–3½″ long, 1″–1½″ wide; flowers white, with 5 elongated petals ½″–¾″ long; fruits fleshy, red, ¼″–½″ in diameter. Ht. 10′–40′; diam. 6″–24″. **Habitat:** Woods, along streams, on rocky bluffs. **Comment:** Roundleaf serviceberry, *A. sanguinea*, has coarsely toothed leaves, petals less than ½″ long, and red twigs.

Prairie Crab Apple, *Malus ioensis*

Field Marks: Leaves simple, ovate, irregularly toothed to shallowly lobed, hairy on the lower surface, 2″–4″ long, 1″–1½″ wide; branchlets with sharp spines, densely hairy when young; flowers several in a cluster, 1¼″–2″ across, with 5 pink or white petals; fruits spherical, yellow-green apples 1″–1½″ in diameter. Ht. 10′–25′; diam. 4″–15″. **Habitat:** Prairies, open woods, fields.

American Plum

American Mountain-ash

Downy Serviceberry

Prairie Crab Apple

HAWTHORNS, CATCLAW ACACIA, SILKTREE

Leaves alternate, deciduous.

Cockspur Thorn, *Crataegus crus-galli*

Field Marks: Branchlets bearing stout spines; leaves simple, widest near the tip, tapering to the base, toothed but without lobes, smooth, shiny on the upper surface, 1½″–2½″ long, ½″–1¼″ wide; flowers several in a cluster, each with 5 white or pink petals; fruits fleshy, red, spherical, ¼″–½″ in diameter. Ht. 8′–24′; diam. 4″–10″. **Habitat:** Woods and thickets. **Comment:** Frosted hawthorn, *C. pruinosa*, has smooth leaves that are sometimes lobed and widest near the base.

Downy Hawthorn, *Crataegus mollis*

Field Marks: Branchlets sometimes bearing stout spines; leaves simple, widest near the base, toothed as well as shallowly lobed, densely hairy on the lower surface, 2″–5″ long, 1½″–3½″ wide; flowers several in a cluster, each with 5 white petals; fruits fleshy, red, spherical, about ½″ in diameter. Ht. 10′–40′; diam. 5″–15″. **Habitat:** Woods and thickets. **Comment:** Scarlet hawthorn, *C. coccinea*, is similar, but only the veins on the lower surface of the leaves are hairy.

Catclaw Acacia, *Acacia greggii*

Field Marks: Branchlets bearing short, curved, claw-like spines; leaves doubly pinnately compound, with 20–40 smooth, toothless leaflets about ¼″ long; pods flat but twisted, 2″–5″ long. Ht. 10′–25′; diam. 4″–12″. **Habitat:** Dry soil, in sand, in grasslands, on mesas.

Silktree, *Albizia julibrissin*

Field Marks: Branchlets without spines; leaves doubly pinnately compound, with up to 200 leaflets; each leaflet smooth, toothless, about ¼″ long; flowers crowded into pink "powderpuff" clusters; pods flat, 3″–8″ long, ¾″–1½″ broad. Ht. 15′–50′; diam. 6″–18″. **Habitat:** This introduced species is found along roads where it has escaped from cultivation.

Cockspur Thorn

Downy Hawthorn

Catclaw Acacia

Silktree

MESQUITES, REDBUD,
HONEYLOCUST, COFFEETREE

Leaves alternate, deciduous.

Mesquite, *Prosopis velutina*

Field Marks: Branchlets with spines up to 2″ long; leaves doubly pinnately compound, with up to 40 leaflets; each leaflet narrowly elliptical, hairy, toothless, ¼″–½″ long, less than ¼″ wide; flowers yellow-green, borne in spikes 2″–3″ long; pods flat, straight, 4″–7″ long, ¼″–¾″ wide. Ht. 10′–35′; diam. 6″–30″. **Habitat:** Rocky soils. **Comment:** Screwbean mesquite, *P. pubescens*, has pods twisted into screw-shaped spirals.

Eastern Redbud, *Cercis canadensis*

Field Marks: Leaves simple, thin, broadly ovate, heart-shaped at the base, without teeth, usually somewhat hairy on the lower surface, 3″–6″ long and about as wide; flowers sweet-pea-shaped, pink, about ½″ long, borne in clusters on the trunk and older branches; pods flat, 3″–6″ long, ¼″–¾″ broad. Ht. 10′–30′; diam. 4″–12″. **Habitat:** Woods.

Honeylocust, *Gleditsia triacanthos*

Field Marks: Trunks often with large, 3-branched spines; leaves usually doubly pinnately compound, with up to 100 leaflets; each leaflet lanceolate, without teeth, smooth, ½″–1½″ long, ¼″–½″ wide; pods long, narrow, flat and often twisted, purple-brown to dark brown, 6″–18″ long, 1″–1½″ wide. Ht. 40′–100′; diam. 8″–42″. **Habitat:** Wet soil along streams and in woods.

Kentucky Coffeetree, *Gymnocladus dioicus*

Field Marks: Trunk and branches not spiny; leaves doubly pinnately compound, with up to 65 leaflets; each leaflet broadly lanceolate, without teeth, smooth or hairy, 1¾″–2½″ long, ¾″–1¼″ wide; pods thick, flat, 5″–9″ long, 1½″–2½″ wide. Ht. 40′–100′; diam. 10″–42″. **Habitat:** Rich woods.

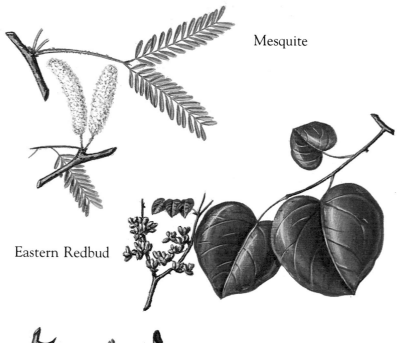

Mesquite

Eastern Redbud

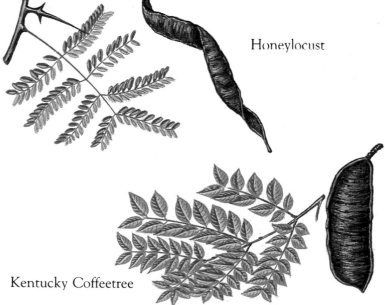

Honeylocust

Kentucky Coffeetree

PALOVERDES, YELLOWWOOD, MESCALBEAN, BLACK LOCUST

Leaves alternate, pinnately compound.

Yellow Paloverde, *Cercidium microphyllum*

Field Marks: Branchlets spiny; leaves doubly pinnately compound, deciduous, with 20–24 leaflets; each leaflet yellow-green, without teeth, smooth, about ¼" long; flowers in small clusters, pale yellow, about ½" across; pods 1½"–4" long, ¼"–½" wide. Ht. 8'–20'; diam. 4"–10". **Habitat:** Deserts. **Comment:** Blue paloverde, *C. floridum*, has blue-green leaves.

Yellowwood, *Clarastis kentukea*

Field Marks: Branchlets without spines; leaves deciduous, pinnately divided, with 5–11 leaflets; each leaflet broadly elliptical, without teeth, smooth, 2½"–4" long, 1½"–2½" wide; flowers white, ¾"–1" long, in long hanging clusters; pods flat, 2"–3" long. Ht. 20'–60'; diam. 10"–24". **Habitat:** Rich woods.

Mescalbean, *Sophora secundiflora*

Field Marks: Branchlets without spines; leaves evergreen, pinnately compound, with 5–9 leaflets; each leaflet elliptical, leathery, without teeth, smooth, 1"–2½" long, ½"–1½" wide; flowers blue-purple, ¾" long, in elongated clusters; pods woody, constricted between the seeds, 1½"–5" long. Ht. 8'–35'; diam. 4"–10". **Habitat:** Often along streams.

Black Locust, *Robinia pseudoacacia*

Field Marks: Branchlets with a pair of short, sharp spines where each leaf is attached; leaves deciduous, pinnately compound, with 7–19 leaflets; each leaflet broadly elliptical, without teeth, smooth, 1¼"–2" long, ½"–¾" wide; flowers cream white, fragrant, about 1" long, in hanging clusters; pods flat, red-brown, 3" 4" long, about ½" wide. Ht. 15'–60'; diam. 10"–45". **Habitat:** Woods; often along roads.

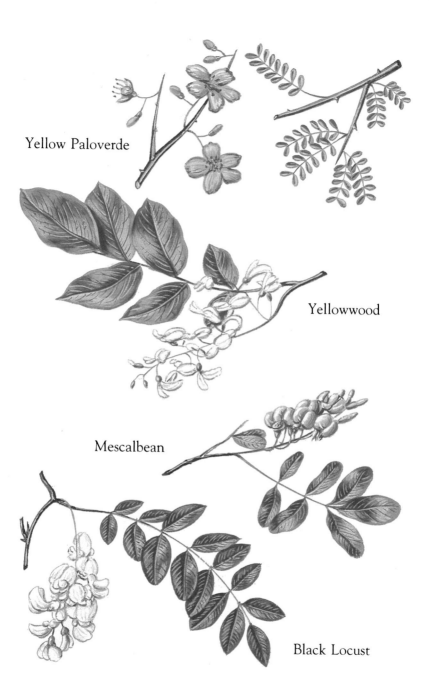

Yellow Paloverde

Yellowwood

Mescalbean

Black Locust

DESERT IRONWOOD, BLUEGUM, DOGWOODS

Desert Ironwood, *Olneya tesota*

Field Marks: Branchlets bearing pairs of slender spines; leaves deciduous, once pinnately compound, with 14–20 leaflets; each leaflet gray to blue-green, rounded at the tip, without teeth, ¼″ long; flowers rose-purple, sweet-pea-shaped, few in a cluster; pods somewhat constricted between the seeds, 1½″–2½″ long, with sticky hairs. Ht. 8′–30′; diam. 6″–24″. **Habitat:** Sandy hills and mesas.

Bluegum, *Eucalyptus globulus*

Field Marks: Bark of the trunk peeling in long shreds; leaves evergreen, alternate, simple, curved, sickle-shaped, without teeth, smooth, 4″–7″ long, ¾″–1″ wide; fruits woody, 4-parted. Ht. 40′–250′; diam. 1′–4′. **Habitat:** An introduced species, this tree is now found along roadsides.

Flowering Dogwood, *Cornus florida*

Field Marks: Leaves deciduous, simple, opposite, ovate, deeply veined, without teeth, hairy and paler on the lower surface, 2½″–6″ long, 1½″–2″ wide; flower clusters with 4 white petal-like structures (bracts) notched at the tip; berries red, shiny, oblong, ½″ long. Ht. 10′–45′; diam. 6″–20″. **Habitat:** Woods.

Pacific Dogwood, *Cornus nuttallii*

Field Marks: Leaves deciduous, simple, opposite, ovate, deeply veined, paler and usually hairy on the lower surface, 2½″–6″ long, 1½″–2″ wide; flower clusters with 5 or 6 petal-like structures (bracts) pointed at the tip; berries red or orange, egg-shaped, ½″ long. Ht. 20′–100′; diam. 8″–30″. **Habitat:** Rich woods.

Desert Ironwood

fruit

Bluegum

Flowering Dogwood

Pacific Dogwood

TUPELO, BLACKGUM, HOLLIES

Leaves alternate, simple.

Water Tupelo, *Nyssa aquatica*

Field Marks: Leaves deciduous, oblong, pointed at the tip, without teeth or irregularly toothed, paler and hairy on the lower surface, 4″–9″ long, 2″–5″ wide; fruits fleshy, elliptical, dark purple, 1″–1½″ long. Ht. 30′–120′; diam. 1′–5′. **Habitat:** Swamps, sometimes in standing water.

Blackgum, *Nyssa sylvatica*

Field Marks: Leaves deciduous, ovate to elliptical, pointed at the tip, without teeth or sometimes with 1 or 2 irregular teeth, smooth or hairy on the lower surface, 2½″–6″ long, ½″–4″ wide; fruits fleshy, slightly longer than they are wide, dark blue, about ½″ long. Ht. 20′–110′; diam. 10″–4½′. **Habitat:** Woods.

American Holly, *Ilex opaca*

Field Marks: Leaves evergreen, widest near the middle, with coarse and prickly teeth, leathery, usually smooth, ½″–3½″ long, ¾″–2″ wide; fruits fleshy, spherical, red, ¼″–½″ in diameter. Ht. 15′–50′; diam. 8″–26″. **Habitat:** Rich woods. **Comment:** Large gallberry, *I. coriacea*, has fewer spine-tipped teeth on the leaves and has black berries.

Possumhaw, *Ilex decidua*

Field Marks: Leaves deciduous, elliptical, tapering to each end, with tiny round teeth, paler and smooth on the lower surface, 1″–3″ long, ½″–1″ wide; fruits fleshy, spherical, usually red, ¼″ in diameter. Ht. 10′–30′; diam. 4″–8″. **Habitat:** Wet soil, but occasionally growing in uplands.

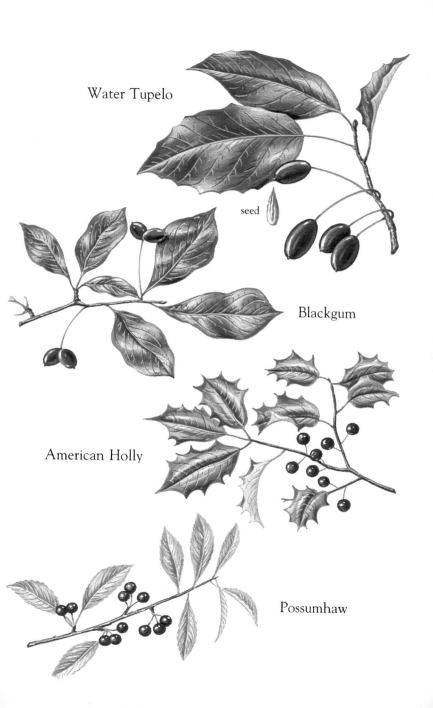

Water Tupelo

seed

Blackgum

American Holly

Possumhaw

BUCKTHORN, RAINTREE, SOAPBERRY, BUCKEYES

Leaves deciduous.

Carolina Buckthorn, *Rhamnus caroliniana*

Field Marks: Leaves alternate, simple, elliptical, with or without very small, rounded teeth, smooth or hairy on the lower surface, 2″–4½″ long, 1″–2″ wide; fruits fleshy, spherical, black, about ¼″ in diameter. Ht. 10′–40′; diam. 4″–8″. **Habitat:** Rich woods.

Golden Raintree, *Koelreuteria paniculata*

Field Marks: Leaves alternate, singly or doubly pinnately compound, with 7–17 leaflets; each leaflet lanceolate to ovate, coarsely toothed or even shallowly lobed, smooth, 1″–3″ long, ¾″–2″ wide; flowers yellow, small, but numerous in large clusters; fruits papery, 3-angled, 1″–2″ long. Ht. 10′–50′; diam. 6″–18″. **Habitat:** Cities. An introduced species, it often seeds and spreads.

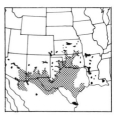

Western Soapberry, *Sapindus drummondii*

Field Marks: Leaves alternate, pinnately compound, with 7–19 leaflets; each leaflet lanceolate, curved, pointed at the tip, asymmetrical at the base, toothed, hairy on the lower surface, 1½″–4″ long, less than 1″ wide; fruits fleshy, spherical, yellow, about ½″ in diameter. Ht. 10′–50′; diam. 8″–30″. **Habitat:** Dry woods.

Ohio Buckeye, *Aesculus glabra*

Field Marks: Leaves opposite, palmately compound, with usually 5 leaflets; each leaflet lanceolate to elliptical, pointed at the tip, tapering to the base, toothed, usually smooth on the lower surface, 4″–6″ long, 1″–2″ wide; buds not sticky; flowers yellow-green, ½″–1″ long, in elongated clusters; fruits are capsules 1″–2″ in diameter, each covered by a leathery, short-spined husk and containing 1 or 2 large red-brown seeds. Ht. 20′–80′; diam. 8″–36″. **Habitat:** Moist or rich woods. **Comment:** Yellow buckeye, *A. octandra*, is very similar, but the fruits are not spiny.

102

Carolina Buckthorn

Golden Raintree

Western Soapberry

Ohio Buckeye

HORSECHESTNUT, MAPLES

Leaves opposite, deciduous.

Horsechestnut, *Aesculus hippocastanum*

Field Marks: Leaves palmately compound, with usually 7 leaflets; each leaflet widest above the middle, tapering to the base, toothed, usually smooth, 4″–10″ long, 1½″–3″ wide; buds sticky; flowers white, 1″–1½″ long, in large clusters; fruits in the form of capsules 1″–2″ in diameter, each covered by a leathery, short-spined husk and containing 1 or 2 large dark brown seeds. Ht. 25′–75′; diam. 10″–2′. **Habitat:** An introduced species, sometimes found where trees planted in cities have seeded and spread.

Bigleaf Maple, *Acer macrophyllum*

Field Marks: Leaves simple, deeply palmately 5-lobed, paler and smooth on the lower surface, 5″–12″ long and about as wide, with milky sap; fruits 1″–1½″ long, 2-winged, with the wings not widely spread. Ht. 30′–100′; diam. 10″–3′. **Habitat:** Rich woods. **Comment:** Vine maple, *A. circinatum*, has leaves with 7–9 shallow lobes and more widely spreading 2-winged fruits.

Striped Maple, *Acer pensylvanicum*

Field Marks: Leaves simple, shallowly 3-lobed, toothed, smooth, 3″–6″ long and about as wide, *without* milky sap; fruits ¾″–1″ long, 2-winged, with wings spreading wide. Ht. 10′–40′; diam. 4″–15″. **Habitat:** Rich woods. **Comment:** Mountain maple, *A. spicatum*, also has shallowly 3-lobed leaves, but the leaves are hairy on the lower surface; the 2-winged fruits are not widely spreading.

Norway Maple, *Acer platanoides*

Field Marks: Leaves simple, with 5 or 7 lobes, 3″–6″ long and nearly as wide, with milky sap; fruits 1½″–2″ long, 2-winged, with wings spreading wide. Ht. 30′–100′; diam. 10″–3′. **Habitat:** Native to Europe, this species is sometimes found where trees planted in cities have seeded and spread. **Comment:** Another European maple sometimes cultivated is the sycamore maple, *A. pseudoplatanus*, which lacks milky sap and does not have widely spreading, 2-winged fruits.

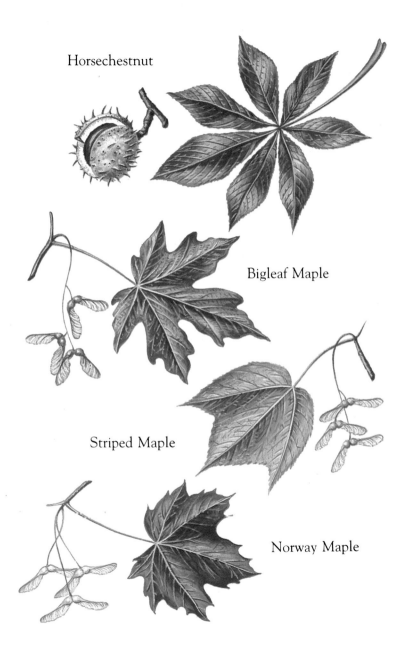

Horsechestnut

Bigleaf Maple

Striped Maple

Norway Maple

MAPLES

Leaves opposite, simple, deciduous.

Rocky Mountain Maple, *Acer glabrum*

Field Marks: Leaves with 3 or 5 usually shallow lobes, toothed, smooth, 3″–6″ long and about as wide; fruits ¾″–1″ long, 2-winged, with wings not widely spread. Ht. 10′–30′; diam. 6″–15″. **Habitat:** Moist woods. **Comment:** Bigtooth maple, *A. grandidentatum*, has more deeply lobed leaves that are hairy on the lower surface.

Red Maple, *Acer rubrum*

Field Marks: Leaves with 3 or 5 usually shallow lobes, toothed, paler and usually smooth on the lower surface, 2″–5″ long and nearly as wide; fruits ½″–1″ long, 2-winged, with wings not widely spread. Ht. 30′–85′; diam. 1′–5′. **Habitat:** Both moist and dry woods.

Silver Maple, *Acer saccharinum*

Field Marks: Leaves with 5 deep lobes, toothed, paler but smooth on the lower surface, 5″–8″ long, 4″–7″ wide; fruits 1½″–3″ long, 2-winged, with wings not widely spread. Ht. 35′–100′; diam. 1′–3½′. **Habitat:** Wet soil, often along streams.

Black Maple, *Acer nigrum*

Field Marks: Leaves with 3 or 5 lobes, toothed, hairy on the lower surface, 4″–8″ long and about as wide; fruits ½″–1″ long, 2-winged, with wings not widely spread. Ht. 30′–75′; diam. 1′–4′. **Habitat:** Rich woods.

Rocky Mountain Maple

Red Maple

Silver Maple

Black Maple

MAPLES, SUMACS

Leaves deciduous.

Sugar Maple, *Acer saccharum*
Field Marks: Leaves opposite, simple, with 3 or 5 lobes and a few coarse teeth, smooth or hairy on the lower surface, 4"–8" long and about as wide; fruits 1"–1½" long, 2-winged, with wings not widely spread. Ht. 35'–100'; diam. 1'–6'. **Habitat:** Rich woods.

Boxelder, *Acer negundo*
Field Marks: Leaves opposite, pinnately compound, with 3 or 5 leaflets; each leaflet toothed, smooth or hairy on the lower surface, 2"–5" long, 1½"–3" wide; fruits 1½"–2" long, 2-winged, with several hanging in a cluster and wings not widely spread. Ht. 25'–75'; diam. 10"–4'. **Habitat:** Wet soil.

Smooth Sumac, *Rhus glabra*
Field Marks: Leaves alternate, pinnately compound with 11–31 leaflets; each leaflet lanceolate, toothed, paler and hairy on the lower surface, 2"–3½" long, ½"–1" wide; fruits in the form of large clusters of spherical, hairy, dark red berries, each less than ¼" in diameter. Ht. 8'–30'; diam. 2"–4". **Habitat:** Fields, thickets, moist areas. **Comment:** Staghorn sumac, *R. typhina*, has densely hairy twigs.

Shining Sumac, *Rhus copallina*
Field Marks: Leaves alternate, pinnately compound with 9–21 leaflets; each leaflet lanceolate to elliptical, sometimes with shallow teeth, very shiny on the upper surface, paler and hairy on the lower surface, 1½"–2½" long, ¾"–1" wide, attached to a winged stalk; fruits in the form of large clusters of nearly spherical, hairy, dark red berries, each less than ¼" in diameter. Ht. 8'–30'; diam. 2" 5". **Habitat:** Fields, thickets.

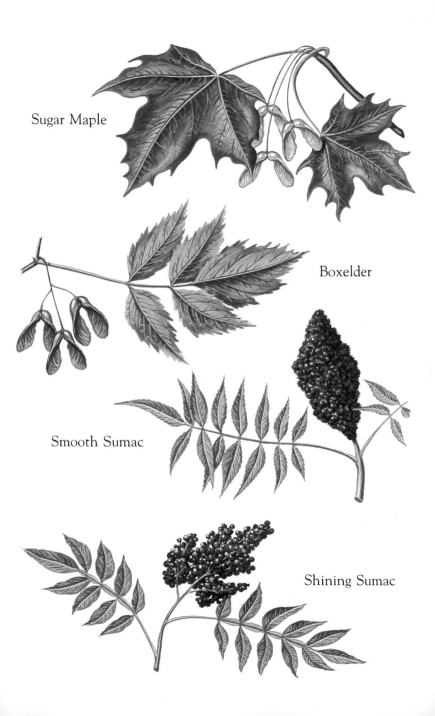

Sugar Maple

Boxelder

Smooth Sumac

Shining Sumac

AILANTHUS, PRICKLY-ASH, CHINABERRY, DEVILS-WALKINGSTICK

Leaves alternate, pinnately compound, deciduous.

Ailanthus, *Ailanthus altissima*

Field Marks: Leaves with 11–41 leaflets; each leaflet lanceolate, pointed at the tip, usually with 2 or more coarse teeth near the base, smooth and paler on the lower surface; seed in the middle of a thin, twisted, pink or yellow wing 1½″–2½″ long. Ht. 30′–75′; diam. 1′–4′. **Habitat:** An introduced species often planted in cities, this tree is now found along roads and in woods.

Prickly-ash, *Zanthoxylum americanum*

Field Marks: Branches with short, stiff spines often in pairs; leaves with 5–11 leaflets; each leaflet lanceolate, pointed at the tip, without teeth or sometimes with a few teeth, smooth or hairy and paler on the lower surface, 1¼″–2½″ long, ½″–¾″ wide; fruits in the form of clusters of tiny, spherical, red-brown capsules about ¼″ in diameter. Ht. 10′–35′; diam. 4″–8″. **Habitat:** Moist or dry woods, sometimes forming thickets.

Chinaberry, *Melia azederach*

Field Marks: Leaves doubly pinnately compound, with 35–51 leaflets; each leaflet lanceolate, pointed at the tip, toothed, smooth, 1″–2¼″ long, ½″–¾″ wide; flowers several in a cluster, purple, with 5 or 6 narrow petals; fruits fleshy, spherical, yellow, ½″–¾″ in diameter. Ht. 15′–50′; diam. 6″–2′. **Habitat:** An introduced species, this tree is now found in fields, along roadsides, and on lawns.

Devils-walkingstick, *Aralia spinosa*

Field Marks: Branches densely prickly; leaves doubly pinnately compound, with many leaflets; each leaflet lanceolate, pointed at the tip, toothed, smooth and paler on the lower surface, 2″–3″ long, 1¼″–1¼″ wide; flowers small, white, in huge clusters; berries spherical, black, about ¼″ in diameter. Ht. 8′–25′; diam. 4″–10″. **Habitat:** Woods.

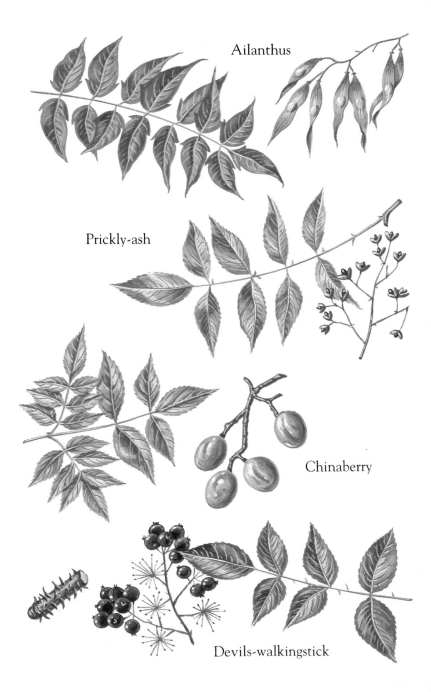

Ailanthus

Prickly-ash

Chinaberry

Devils-walkingstick

OLEANDER, DEVILWOOD,
FRINGETREE, SWAMP-PRIVET

Leaves opposite, simple.

Oleander, *Nerium oleander*

Field Marks: Leaves with a milky sap, deciduous, lanceolate, pointed at the tip, without teeth, 2″–5″ long, ½″–¾″ wide; flowers tubular and white, pink, or purple. Ht. 10′–35′; diam. 3″–6″. **Habitat:** An introduced species, this tree is now found along roadsides.

Devilwood, *Osmanthus americanus*

Field Marks: Leaves evergreen, elliptical, pointed at the tip, without teeth, smooth and paler on the lower surface, 3½″–5½″ long, 1″–2½″ wide; fruits fleshy, spherical, dark blue, about ½″ in diameter. Ht. 15′–50′; diam. 4″–1′. **Habitat:** Rich woods.

Fringetree, *Chionanthus virginicus*

Field Marks: Leaves deciduous, elliptical, pointed at the tip, without teeth, smooth or hairy and always paler on the lower surface, 4″–8″ long, ¾″–3½″ wide; flowers numerous, borne in large clusters, each flower with 4 white petals ¾″–1¼″ long. Ht. 8′–30′; diam. 3″–8″. **Habitat:** Rich woods.

Swamp-privet, *Forestiera acuminata*

Field Marks: Leaves deciduous, widest at the middle, tapering to each end, shallowly toothed, smooth and paler on the lower surface, 2″–4½″ long, 1″–1¼″ wide; fruits fleshy, oblong, dark purple, ½″–1″ long. Ht. 8′–30′; diam. 2″–5″. **Habitat:** Along rivers; wet soil.

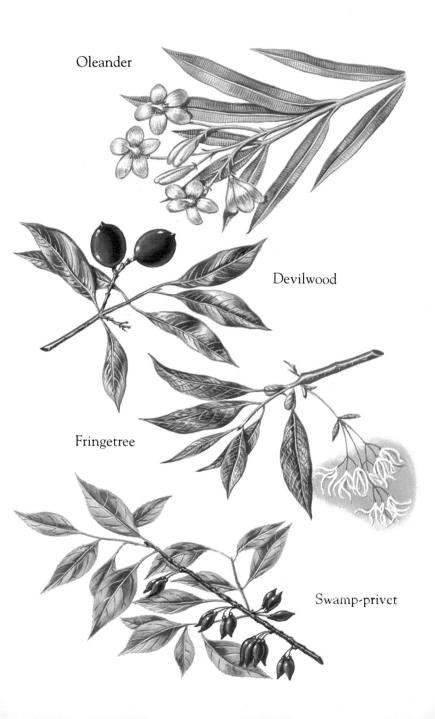

Oleander

Devilwood

Fringetree

Swamp-privet

ASHES

Leaves opposite, pinnately compound, deciduous.

Blue Ash, *Fraxinus quadrangulata*

Field Marks: Branchlets square; leaves with 5–11 leaflets; each leaflet lanceolate, pointed at the tip, toothed, smooth or hairy and paler on the lower surface, 3″–5″ long, 1″–2″ wide; fruits 1-seeded, winged, 1″–2″ long, ¼″–½″ wide. Ht. 20′–75′; diam. 6″–3′. **Habitat:** Dry woods, usually in limestone areas.

Green Ash, *Fraxinus pennsylvanica*

Field Marks: Leaves with 7–9 leaflets; each leaflet lanceolate, pointed at the tip, smooth or hairy and sometimes paler on the lower surface, finely toothed or sometimes nearly toothless, 3″–5½″ long, ½″–1¼″ wide; fruits 1-seeded, winged, 1″–2½″ long, ¼″–½″ broad. Ht. 30′–75′; diam. 8″–2′. **Habitat:** Woods.

White Ash, *Fraxinus americana*

Field Marks: Leaves with 5–9 leaflets; each leaflet lanceolate to widest near the middle, pointed at the tip, usually finely toothed, smooth or hairy and much paler on the lower surface, 2½″–5½″ long, 1½″–2¾″ wide; fruits 1-seeded, winged, 1¼″–2½″ long, ¼″–½″ wide. Ht. 30′–110′; diam. 1′–6′. **Habitat:** Rich woods.

Pumpkin Ash, *Fraxinus profunda*

Field Marks: Leaves with 5–9 leaflets; each leaflet broadly lanceolate to ovate, pointed at the tip, hairy and paler on the lower surface, 5″–10″ long, 1½″–4½″ wide; fruits 1-seeded, winged, 2″–3″ long, ¼″–½″ wide. Ht. 35′–110′; diam. 1′–5′. **Habitat:** Swamps, wet woods.

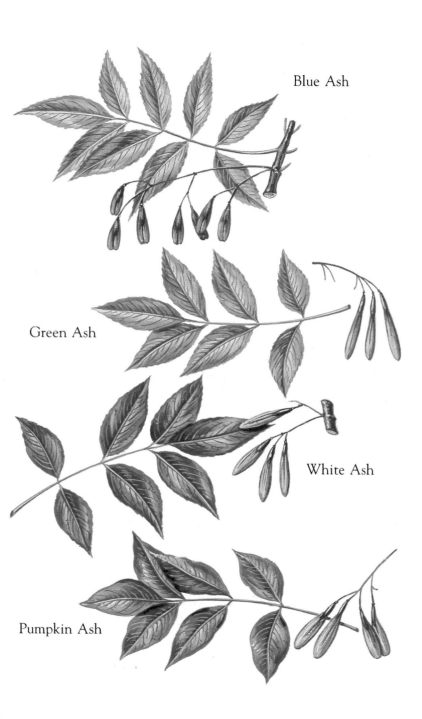

Blue Ash

Green Ash

White Ash

Pumpkin Ash

ASH, PAULOWNIA, CATALPA, DESERT-WILLOW

Leaves deciduous.

Black Ash, *Fraxinus nigra*

Field Marks: Leaves opposite, pinnately compound with 7–11 leaflets; each leaflet lanceolate, pointed at the tip, toothed, somewhat hairy and paler on the lower surface, 3½″–5½″ long, 1¼″–2½″ wide; fruits 1-seeded, winged, 1″–1½″ long, about ¼″ wide. Ht. 25′–65′; diam. 6″–20″. **Habitat:** Swamps; bogs; wet ground.

Royal Paulownia, *Paulownia tomentosa*

Field Marks: Leaves opposite, simple, ovate, heart-shaped at the base, without teeth, hairy, 6″–12″ long, 4″–10″ wide; flowers lavender, 1½″–2½″ long, borne in huge clusters; capsules egg-shaped, brown, hairy, 1½″–2½″ long. Ht. 20′–60′; diam. 8″–2′. **Habitat:** This native of Asia is found along roads.

Northern Catalpa, *Catalpa speciosa*

Field Marks: Leaves opposite or whorled, simple, ovate, heart-shaped at the base, usually without teeth, hairy, 6″–12″ long, 3″–7″ wide; flowers mostly white, 1½″–2½″ long, borne in elongated clusters of a few flowers each; fruits elongated, cylindrical, brown, up to 2′ long, ½″–¾″ wide, containing winged seeds. Ht. 35′–100′; diam. 1′–3′. **Habitat:** Wet soil in woods.

Desert-willow, *Chilopsis linearis*

Field Marks: Leaves alternate, simple, very long and narrow, without teeth, smooth, 3″–6″ long, about ¼″ wide; flowers pink, pale purple, or white, 1″–1½″ long; fruits elongated, cylindrical, brown, 4″–12″ long, containing winged seeds. Ht. 8′–35′; diam. 2″–10″. **Habitat:** Dry rocky soil, often along washes.

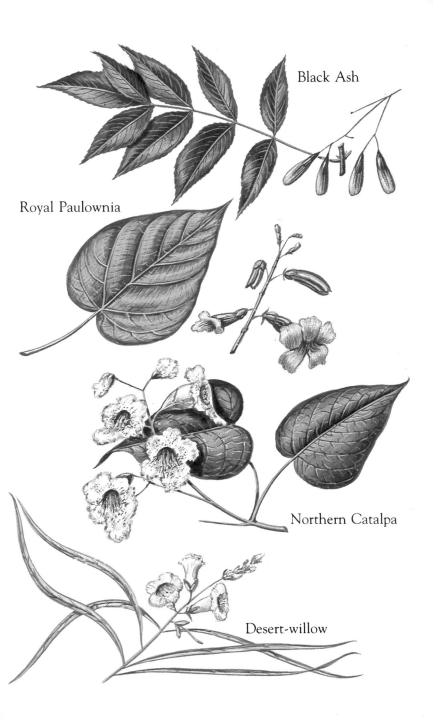

Black Ash

Royal Paulownia

Northern Catalpa

Desert-willow

VIBURNUMS, PALMS

Rusty Blackhaw, *Viburnum rufidulum*

Field Marks: Leaves opposite, simple, widest at the middle, toothed, with rusty hairs on the lower surface, 1½″–3″ long, ¾″–2″ wide; fruits fleshy, dark blue or black, about ½″ long, longer than wide. Ht. 8′–30′; diam. 3″–15″. **Habitat:** Moist woods. **Comment:** Possumhaw viburnum, *V. nudum*, has nearly toothless leaves.

Blackhaw, *Viburnum prunifolium*

Field Marks: Leaves opposite, simple, widest at the middle, toothed, without rusty hairs, 1½″–3″ long, ¾″–2″ wide; fruits fleshy, dark blue or black, about ½″ long, longer than wide. Ht. 8′–35′; diam. 3″–12″. **Habitat:** Moist woods.

Coconut Palm, *Cocos nucifera*

Field Marks: Trunk curved; leaves very large, confined to the top of the trunk, up to 15′ long, with numerous narrow leaflets; coconuts up to 10″ long. Ht. 25′–60′; diam. 10″–20″. **Habitat:** An introduced species, this tree is now found along shores in warm climates.

Cabbage Palmetto, *Sabal palmetto*

Field Marks: Trunk straight; leaves fan-shaped, up to 6′ long, wider than long, divided into many narrow segments; fruits fleshy, spherical, black, ¼″–½″ in diameter. Ht. 25′–75′; diam. 10″–20″. **Habitat:** Marshes, wet woods. **Comment:** Dwarf palmetto, *S. minor*, grows only to a height of 10′.

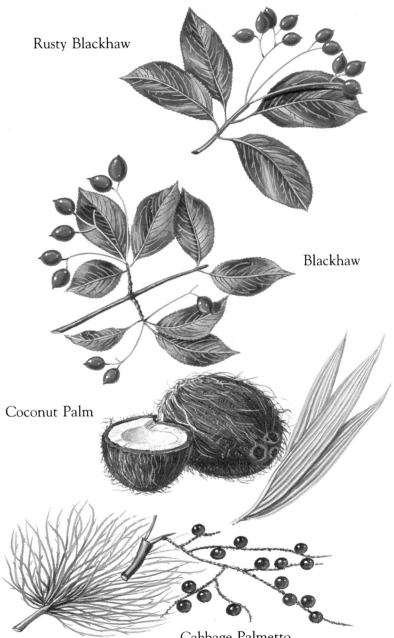

Rusty Blackhaw

Blackhaw

Coconut Palm

Cabbage Palmetto

Further Comments on Conifers

John W. Thieret

Page 4—California Torreya, Pacific Yew, Redwood, Baldcypress

California torreya is often called California-nutmeg—the kernel of its seed is nutmeg-like. The hard seeds of Pacific yew are toxic, but the pulpy cup in which each seed is borne is edible, though insipid. Birds, fond of the pulp, are important in dispersing the seeds. Redwood, the world's tallest tree and one important for lumber, may grow as high as about 370' and have a diameter of 21'; it is exceeded in volume only by giant sequoia. It can attain an impressive age, too: the oldest known individual lived 2,200 years. Handsome in foliage and form, redwood is a fine ornamental. Its generic name, *Sequoia*, honors Sequoya, the American Indian who devised the Cherokee alphabet in the early 19th century. Baldcypress, its branches often draped with Spanish-moss, is well known in the southeastern United States. It is unusual among conifers in that it drops its leaves, still attached to small twigs, in the fall. The tree is grown for its landscape value well to the north of its natural range. In far southern Texas occurs a similar species, Montezuma baldcypress (*Taxodium mucronatum*).

Pages 6 and 8—Firs

Firs are conical, often spire-like, evergreens with trunks that run straight to the tree's tip; the bark, when young and smooth, is beset with resin "blisters." On top branches, and often best seen with binoculars, are erect, cylindrical to barrel-shaped or egg-shaped cones. At maturity, their scales drop, but the peg-like central stalk remains as a "spike" on the branch.

Fraser fir is common in high-elevation Appalachian forests, often with red spruce. The recent dieback of many of these trees is under study. Balsam fir, the widest-ranging American fir, is a source of pulpwood; it and Fraser fir are popular Christmas trees. Pacific silver fir reaches its zenith in the evergreen forests of Washington's Cascade Mountains. Its common name recalls the silvery undersurface of the leaves. Grand fir, the second tallest American fir, reaches about 230'.

Subalpine fir has the greatest north-south distribution (some 2,400 miles) of any American fir but is of minor commercial value. The silhouette of healthy, mature trees is distinctive—narrowly conical, long-tapering to the tip. Near timberline, though, subalpine fir may be reduced to a gnarled, even prostrate, shrub. White fir, the most important of western firs and much grown as an ornamental, is at its best on western slopes of the Sierra Nevada. It is "white" because the leaves have a whitish cast and the bark is pale. California red fir, with bark sometimes rusty red, bears cones that may grow longer (up to 9″) than those of other American firs. Bark gathered from dead trees was used in the Firefall, a ritual of yesteryear at Yosemite National Park: an embered mound of bark was thrust over a 3000′ cliff after dark, creating a fiery cascade and landing on a ledge 1000′ below. Noble fir is a titan among American firs; a tree in Washington towers to 278′ and has a trunk 28′ in circumference. Logging has decimated many wild stands of the species, but extensive plantings of noble fir have been made for future harvest of lumber.

Page 10—Douglas-fir, Hemlocks

Douglas-fir is exceeded in size among North American trees only by giant sequoia and redwood. It is the continent's most important timber tree. Its name commemorates David Douglas, a Scot who in 1827 sent seeds of this species to Europe, where, as in North America, it is much grown.

Eastern hemlock is a widely used ornamental in many varieties, among them weeping, dwarf, stiffly upright, and prostrate. Its tip shoot curves or droops away from the vertical, a good earmark for all hemlocks. Mountain hemlock, a well-formed tree at lower elevations, may be dwarfed to a low, sprawling shrub at timberline. Karl Mertens, the tree's "discoverer," is remembered in the scientific name. Western hemlock is a major timber and pulpwood tree. The largest of American hemlocks, it is the state tree of Washington.

Page 12—Spruces

Identifying a tree as a spruce is easy. Spruces are conical evergreens whose trunk runs straight to the tree's tip. The needles, borne singly, grow on "pegs" that remain, stubble-like, after needle fall. A glance at a leafless twig of a spruce will confirm identification. Spruce cones have either rounded scales (red, black, and white spruces) or rather angular or wedge-shaped ones (Sitka, Engelmann, and blue spruces), the latter kind looking a bit like corn flakes.

Giant among spruces is Sitka spruce: the tallest individual on record towers to 216′ and has a trunk diameter of 16.7′. To see this species in its full stature, visit the forests of Washington's Olympic Peninsula. Red spruce, the common spruce in the mountains of New York and New England, grows largest in the southern Appalachians. It, too, is an important timber tree. Black spruce, valued for pulpwood, is a typical tree of (though not confined to) cold bogs and swamps, often mixed with eastern larch. White spruce, Canada's most important commercial tree, is much used for pulpwood and lumber. It and black spruce both range north to latitudes where trees give way to arctic tundra.

Page 14—Spruces, Larches

The widest-ranging spruce of the West is Engelmann spruce, named for George Engelmann, a 19th-century botanist and physician who first recognized

122

this species as different from other spruces. Though it is common at higher elevations in the Rockies, its relative inaccessibility limits its commercial value. Blue spruce, the state tree of Colorado and Utah, ranks in popularity with the introduced Norway spruce as a tree for landscape use. Cultivated specimens, with their silvery blue foliage, may bear scant resemblance to the tree in its mountain home, where the leaves are often a somber, undistinguished green.

Larches are readily identified by their stubby side twigs ("spurs"), each tipped with many needles. The tips of the twigs, which represent the latest year's growth, have needles borne singly. Larches are one of the few kinds of conifers that drop their needles in fall. The range of eastern larch is transcontinental and extends north to the edge of the treeless arctic. Stands of the tree may be defoliated periodically by insects; such attacks over several years may kill thousands of trees. Western larch is the largest and commercially most important New World larch. Its wood, durable in contact with the soil, is valuable for telephone poles, construction lumber, and plywood.

Page 16—5-Needle Pines

Eastern white pine is the largest northeastern conifer. Although most of the original stands have been logged, the tree reseeds itself well and has been extensively planted. It and the similar western white pine are among the most important temperate North American timber trees. Both are excellent ornamentals for lawns and parks. The largest pine in the world, and also a major timber producer, is sugar pine. The current champion is 216' tall, with a trunk diameter of about 10'. Sugar pine cones are among the largest developed by any conifer. From wounds in the bark of the tree exudes a whitish and sweet resin—thus the name "sugar." Limber pine is of hardly any commercial importance—it is a small tree and its wood is knotty. The "limber" refers to the markedly flexible twigs and smaller branches; one can almost tie a knot in them.

Page 18—5-Needle Pines, Pinyon Pines

Bristlecone pines are well known for their extreme age. The intermountain species can live for at least 4,600–5,000 years. Many of these ancient trees are protected in California's Inyo National Forest. One less fortunate tree, said to have been 5,000 years old, was cut down in Nevada.

Often resembling orchards, forests of pinyon pines cover millions of acres of arid land in the western and southwestern United States. The pines often grow with junipers in a distinctive plant community known as pinyon-juniper woodland, which occurs at elevations above those of the true deserts but below those of the forests of larger pines, spruces, and firs. The seeds of pinyon pines, called pine nuts, were long a staple food of some American Indian tribes and are now considered a delicacy. Single-leaf pinyon is the state tree of Nevada; pinyon, the state tree of New Mexico.

Page 20—**Eastern 2-Needle Pines**

Table-mountain pine, when growing in the open, may have a short trunk almost hidden by horizontal or drooping branches that, heavy with cones, extend nearly to the ground. Trees found in forests, in contrast, typically have a long, clear trunk. Seed production begins as early as the fifth year in this species. The common name recalls one of the pine's habitats—dry-gravelly tablelands of the Appalachians. Two varieties of sand pine can be distinguished. One of these has so-called fire cones, which typically remain closed until heated, as by a fire; great numbers of seeds are then released. The other, less common, has cones that open when mature; some seeds are thus dropped each year. The former occurs in stands of trees of the same age that developed after fires; the latter, in stands with trees of various ages. Spruce pine has bark like that of some oaks: deeply furrowed and dark gray to black. Unlike the seeds of many pines, those of this species germinate well in shade; the species is thus said to be shade-tolerant. Shortleaf pine, a commercially important tree, yields valuable lumber. A significant characteristic of the species is its ability to produce sprouts vigorously from stumps following fire or cutting. Some of these sprouts may grow to harvestable size.

Page 22—**Eastern 2-Needle Pines**

Jack pine is North America's most northerly pine, nearly reaching the arctic circle in northwestern Canada. Many of its cones—the so-called fire cones—may remain closed for up to 25 years, finally opening and shedding their seeds—often still viable—after they have been heated in a forest fire. Following such fires, therefore, jack pine reseeds itself rapidly. Trees of the same age characterize such after-fire forests. The natural range of Scots pine (often called Scotch pine) spans much of northern Eurasia. The tree is important for timber in Europe, but in North America it is used mostly, and extensively, for reforestation. Virginia pine, frequently a scraggly tree, is commonly a pioneer species after fires or an invader of abandoned agricultural land. Such stands are usually replaced in time by other, more competitive trees. The main use of the wood is for paper pulp. Red pine is also known as Norway pine, a geographical misnomer for this North American native. A lumber and pulpwood tree reaching its best development in the Upper Great Lakes region, the tree is much planted for reforestation and for ornament.

Page 24—**Southeastern 2-Needle and 3-Needle Pines**

Longleaf pine is a species important for lumber and for naval stores—turpentine, rosin, and related products. For the first several years of life, during the "grass stage" of the species, longleaf pines produce above ground only a dense, grasslike clump of long needles. Slash pine is also a major source of lumber and naval stores. A rapidly growing tree, it is widely planted for reforestation. In peninsular Florida, some slash pines go through a "grass stage" similar to that of longleaf pine. Loblolly pine, the commonest and leading commercial pine in the southeastern United States, often grows in moist depressions locally called loblollies, hence its common name. It is an invader of cutover or abandoned land and old fields. Pond pine is one of those pines that produce stump shoots, which may develop following fire or cutting. Its wood is used for pulp (one-half of the total U.S. requirement of pulpwood comes from the southeastern pines) and for construction.

Page 26—**Western Pines**

The heaviest cones produced by any North American pine are those of Coulter pine, which may weigh 4–6 pounds when green. Falling from the tree, they can be dangerous objects. These cones, because of their many long "claws," have been well described as "horribly armed." The large seeds are edible. Digger pine, too, produces large, edible seeds, which were an important food for the so-called Digger Indians of California. Because of the tree's sparse needles, it has been said that one can "see right through" a Digger pine. The big cones are the second heaviest of any pine in North America. And they, also, are impressively "armed"; they are even a bit uncomfortable to handle. One of the most familiar trees of the West, and one of the most wide ranging of American pines, ponderosa pine is of major importance as a source of lumber. The tree is long-lived; the oldest individual accurately studied was found to have 726 annual rings. A 5-needle variety of ponderosa pine occurs in southern Arizona and New Mexico and in adjacent Mexico. Jeffrey pine so closely resembles ponderosa pine that the two are not distinguished in the lumber trade. The two trees may occur together. Jeffrey pines may live to be 500 to 600 years old.

Page 28—**Western Pines, Giant Sequoia**

Knobcone pine is another pine that produces "fire cones." These may remain unopened on the tree for years and can even be found still tightly attached to trunks as much as 1 foot in diameter. An abundance of seeds is usually released only after the cones are heated—as by a fire—and then open. The soft, weak wood of this pine is of little importance except locally for fuel. Monterey pine, though occurring naturally in only a few areas along the Pacific coast, is of great value worldwide as an ornamental and timber tree and for reforestation. An estimated 1.5 million acres have been planted with this species. A rapid grower, Monterey pine produces sawtimber in a relatively short time. Plantation-grown trees 30 years old may be 140' tall and 3' in diameter. Lodgepole pine is so called because of the use of its young trunks for tepee poles by American Indians. The seaside form of the species, often of small size and twisted form (hence the scientific name *contorta*), is strikingly different from the tall, straight, slender inland form, which is an important timber tree.

Giant sequoia, the world's largest tree in volume and weight, grows in about 30 groves in the Sierra Nevada. Most sequoias are in areas where they are protected. Ring counts on felled trees show ages up to 3,200 years. The largest giant sequoia in circumference is the General Sherman Tree in Sequoia National Park: 101.6' at 4.5' above the ground. The tallest is the McKinley Tree, which towers 291'.

Page 30—Incense-cedar, White-cedars

The name "cedar" is applied, in temperate North America, to a variety of trees. Features common to these are small, scale-like leaves and aromatic, lightweight, easily worked wood. (The true cedars, genus *Cedrus*, are needle-leaved Old World trees, such as the cedars of Lebanon; some of them are grown as ornamentals in the United States.)

Incense-cedar produces wood much used for pencils. The tree is frequently planted as a beautiful ornamental. When closed to slightly open, the cones simulate a duck's bill. Atlantic white-cedar is the state tree of New Jersey, where it is common in the Pine Barrens region. Its wood is quite resistant to decay; uses include barrels, furniture, and boats. Alaska-cedar was first found by Europeans at Nootka Sound, Vancouver Island—thus the scientific name. The tree may live for an estimated 3,500 years. Port-Orford-cedar is named for the coastal town of Port Orford, near the center of the Oregon stands of the tree. In many varieties the species is much used for ornamental planting. The mid-1800's saw its introduction into Europe. The first seedlings there were grown by Peter Lawson & Sons; the scientific name commemorates these Scottish nurserymen.

Page 32—Thujas, Arizona Cypress, Eastern Redcedar

A commonly used name for the thujas is arbor-vitae, "tree of life," which recalls its medicinal uses in earlier days. Northern white-cedar was probably the first American tree to be grown in Europe. Many varieties of it are used as ornamentals, and it is also an important winter food for white-tailed deer. Western redcedar is one of the large trees of the Pacific Northwest, reaching 200' in height and at least 16' in trunk diameter. Loggers have taken down trees 800 years old; the maximum claimed age is over 1,000 years. The wood, more durable than strong, is popular for shingles and house siding. Arizona cypress is much used as a Christmas tree. Its wood serves locally for posts and poles. Seven other kinds of cypress, occurring in California, are mostly local and rare trees often difficult to identify. The best known of these is Monterey cypress (*Cupressus macrocarpa*), which grows naturally in a coastal strip about 2 miles long but is much planted worldwide as an ornamental. Eastern redcedar is a common invader of abandoned fields. Birds and small mammals, fond of the cones, spread the seeds far and wide. The wood is used for fenceposts and for furniture, especially cedar chests, and the tree is often planted in yards, parks, and cemeteries.

Pages 34 and 36—Western Junipers

Individual species of western junipers are difficult to identify. In areas where more than one species occurs, identification may be troublesome for trees without "berries"; the novice—or anybody else without experience in juniper identification—may sometimes have to be satisfied simply with "juniper" for these.

Junipers can grow in poor, dry soils, often in otherwise barren areas. They are of value to wildlife: their "berries" and foliage are eaten, and the trees

furnish cover, especially valuable in winter. Animals, especially birds, that eat the "berries" disperse the seeds. The "berries" of some junipers (e.g., one-seed, western, and Utah) were used for food by American Indians.

Weedy junipers have taken over millions of acres of overgrazed western rangeland. Costly efforts are needed to clear juniper-invaded areas to improve range conditions for livestock.

Juniper wood is used mainly for fenceposts and fuel. Oils derived from the wood of some species (e.g., Ashe juniper in Texas) are used to scent soaps, air fresheners, and disinfectants.

Several junipers and low-growing pines are the major trees in pinyon-juniper woodland, a distinctive plant community of vast areas in the western United States at elevations above the deserts and below the mountain forests of spruces, firs, and taller pines.

One-seed juniper, sometimes called cherrystone juniper, is New Mexico's commonest juniper. Rocky Mountain juniper is closely related to eastern redcedar, but its "berries" take two years instead of one to mature. Frequently cultivated as an ornamental, the tree is also planted in shelterbelts. The 3,600-year-old Jardine Juniper, in Logan Canyon, Cache County, Utah, is of this species. Ashe juniper, named after the American forester Willard Ashe, often forms almost impenetrable thickets called cedar breaks. Western juniper produces large and widespread roots that help anchor it on the exposed, windswept, high-mountain sites where, often gnarled and grotesque in form, it thrives even in rock crevices.

The unique bark of alligator juniper makes it easy to recognize. This species is the largest juniper in Arizona and New Mexico. Pinchot juniper is sometimes called redberry juniper. Its name honors Gifford Pinchot, the first chief of the United States Forest Service. The commonest juniper in Utah and Nevada is Utah juniper, a species being used more and more for ornament in arid regions. California juniper is notable for its ability to grow well on low, desert slopes and plains.

Further Comments on Hardwoods

Robert H. Mohlenbrock

Page 38—Magnolias

Southern magnolia is a valuable ornamental in warm areas of North America because of its shiny evergreen leaves and large fragrant flowers. Sweetbay loses its leaves in the northern part of its range but is evergreen farther south; it, too, is grown as an ornamental. Cucumbertree has the broadest range of any of the native magnolias. The large leaves clustered at the ends of the branches account for the common name of the umbrella magnolia. All of the magnolias bloom in the spring.

Page 40—Magnolias, Yellow-poplar, Pawpaw, Sassafras

Yellow-poplar is also known as tulip tree and tulip-poplar. It is an important timber tree for general construction and furniture, as well as a fast-growing ornamental. The banana-like fruit of the pawpaw is edible and particularly liked by wildlife. Pawpaw leaves have a bad odor when handled. Related to pawpaw is pond apple, *Annona glabra,* of southern Florida, which has 5"-long edible yellow fruits spotted with brown. Sassafras tea is made from boiling roots of the sassafras, but it has been shown to be carcinogenic. Sassafras leaves turn brilliant colors during the autumn.

Page 42—California-laurel, Redbay, Sycamores

California-laurel, also known as Pacific myrtle, has strongly scented leaves that can be used in cooking. The wood of this species takes a high polish and is valued for making bowls and candlesticks. Redbay is an important ornamental because of its shiny evergreen leaves and its apparent resistance to disease. Its leaves have a spicy odor when crushed. American sycamores are extremely fast-growing and sometimes attain tremendous girths. California sycamore, *Platanus racemosa,* is similar to Arizona sycamore but usually has leaves with only 3 or 5 shallow lobes.

Page 44—Sweetgum, Witch-hazel, Elms

Sweetgum, whose leaves turn a variety of colors in the autumn, is a popular ornamental. The buds are sticky. Witch-hazel has yellow flowers with ribbon-like petals that open during late autumn and early winter. Most parts of the witch-hazel contain an oil used in some liniments. Siberian and Chinese elms are native to Asia but are planted in North America because of their

fast growth and resistance to diseases. Similar to the winged elm is the rock elm, *Ulmus thomasii,* which also has corky-winged twigs; it flowers in spring but has larger leaves. It ranges in the north-central states. Cedar elm, *U. crassifolia,* from eastern Texas to Louisiana and Arkansas, and September elm, *U. serotina,* from Arkansas to Alabama, often have corky-winged twigs, but they both bloom in the autumn.

Page 46—Elms, Water-elm, Hackberry

American elms, with their broadly spreading crowns, make handsome ornamentals, but they are being decimated by the incurable Dutch elm disease. The inner bark of the slippery elm becomes very mucilaginous when chewed. Hackberry is frequently infected by a fungus that causes a dense entanglement of small branchlets known as witches' broom.

Page 48—Hackberries, Mulberries, Osage-orange

Lindheimer's hackberry, *Celtis lindheimeri,* of central Texas, is similar to other hackberries but has white hairs on the undersurface. Netleaf hackberry, *C. reticulata,* which lives in dry habitats from Nebraska and Texas to the Pacific states, has leaves less than 3″ long. The fruits of the red mulberry are sweet and are eaten by humans and wildlife. White mulberry, the food of the silkworm, was introduced into North America in an effort to start a silk industry. Texas mulberry, *Morus microphylla,* is a small tree with leaves less than 2″ long. Osage-orange is also called hedge apple. Osage Indians prized its wood for making bows. Paper mulberry has been introduced from Asia.

Page 50—Butternut, Walnut, Pecan, Hickories

The kernels of the butternut and black walnut are edible. The inner central core of both species, called the pith, is divided by numerous partitions; use this field mark as an easy way to tell this group from hickories. Black walnut has valuable wood. Other North American walnut species are the Arizona walnut, *Juglans major,* with nuts more than 1″ in diameter; southern California walnut, *J. californica,* with nuts less than 1″ in diameter and 9–15 broadly lanceolate leaflets; little walnut, *J. microcarpa,* of Oklahoma, Texas, and New Mexico, with nuts less than 1″ in diameter and 11–25 narrowly lanceolate leaflets; and northern California walnut, *J. hindsii,* with nearly ungrooved nuts. The nuts of the pecan are exceptionally tasty; the wood is prized for cabinets and furniture.

Page 52—Hickories

Shagbark hickory is generally conceded to have the best-flavored nut of any of the hickories. An unusual characteristic of the shellbark hickory is that the leaf stalks persist on the twigs long after the leaflets have fallen. This species is also known as kingnut hickory and rivernut hickory.

Page 54—**Hickories, Beech, Chestnuts**

Scrub hickory, *Carya floridana*, is similar in appearance to black hickory but has tiny glandular dots on the lower surface of the leaflets. Beechnuts and chestnuts are tasty when roasted. Most mature beeches have rotted trunks and are not important timber trees. American chestnut has been virtually eliminated by a fungal infection called chestnut blight. Chinese chestnut, *Castanea mollissima*, which is not affected by chestnut blight, is sometimes planted as an ornamental. Ozark chinkapin, *C. ozarkensis*, found in the Ozark Mountains, is a small tree with leaves 4″–8″ long and hairy on the lower surface. Florida chinkapin, *C. alnifolia*, is a small tree with leaves 2″–4″ long and hairy on the lower surface.

Page 56—**Chinkapin, Tanoak, Oaks**

The abundant cream-colored flowers of the golden chinkapin have a strong fragrance. The bark of the tanoak, rich in tannin, was once valued for its use in the tanning industry. Bur oaks, also called mossycup oaks, sometimes are found in grassy savannas. The kernels of the acorns of the bur oak and overcup oak are edible.

Page 58—**Oaks**

The wood of white oak is valued for furniture and interior finishing; that of post oak is used extensively for fence posts. Lacey oak, *Quercus glaucoides*, of south-central Texas, is a small tree with very shallowly lobed gray-green leaves. Chapman oak, *Q. chapmanii*, from the coastal plains of South Carolina to central Florida, has broad leathery leaves with wavy edges. Oglethorpe oak, *Q. oglethorpensis*, confined to Georgia and South Carolina, has toothless leaves with yellow hairs on the lower surface. Oregon white oak, *Q. garryana*, resembles Gambel oak but has dark green leaves and acorns 1″–2″ long. Mexican blue oak, *Q. oblongifolia*, of southern Arizona, has toothless but wavy-edged blue-green leaves. Havard oak, *Q. havardii*, from western Oklahoma to eastern New Mexico, barely reaches tree size and has coarsely toothed bright green leaves. Sandpaper oak, *Q. pungens*, of southern Texas, New Mexico, and Arizona, has jagged-toothed bright green leaves up to 2″ long and rough to the touch.

Page 60—**Oaks**

Swamp chestnut oak is sometimes called basket oak or cow oak. Another name for chestnut oak is rock chestnut oak. Variation from very narrow to very broad leaves is common in chinkapin oak.

Page 62—**Oaks**

The swollen trunk and wide-spreading crown of the live oak make it a handsome ornamental. Mohr's oak, *Quercus mohriana*, which occurs mostly in eastern New Mexico, Texas, and western Oklahoma, has toothless evergreen leaves lightly hairy on the upper surface. California scrub oak, *Q. dumosa*, has 1″-long evergreen leaves with scalloped edges. Engelmann oak, *Q. engelmannii*, also of California, is similar to the California scrub oak but has leaves 1″–3″ long. The wood of the northern red oak is used for furniture and interior finishing.

Page 64—**Oaks**

The presence of short, sharp-pointed twigs on the branches account for the common name of the pin oak. The leaves of this tree are beautifully colored in the autumn. Nuttall oak, *Quercus nuttallii*, which occurs from Missouri and Tennessee south to Alabama and Texas, is very similar to pin oak but has acorns about 1″ long. Georgia oak, *Q. georgiana*, is a small tree similar to the pin oak except that the leaf tapers to the base. The curved terminal leaf lobes of the southern red oak and turkey oak are distinctive.

Page 66—**Oaks**

California black oak, *Quercus kelloggii*, from California and Oregon, is similar to black oak but has acorns 1″–1½″ long. Leaves of the scarlet oak turn a brilliant red in the autumn. Water oak has highly variable leaves, including some without lobes.

Page 68—**Oaks**

Laurel oak is a popular shade tree in the southern states. Shingle oak was used extensively by the early settlers for shingling their houses. Bluejack oak, *Quercus incana*, from the Carolinas to Florida and west to central Texas, is similar to shingle oak but has blue-green leaves with a maximum length of only 4½″.

Page 70—**Oaks, Hornbeams, Birch**

Chisos oak, *Quercus graciliformis*, of the Big Bend region of Texas, has slender branches, evergreen toothed leaves up to 4″ long, and pointed acorns ¾″ long. Dunn oak, *Q. dunnii*, is a small tree in southern California, Arizona, and New Mexico, with evergreen, coarsely toothed leaves and acorns up to half enclosed by the cup. Silverleaf oak, *Q. hypoleucoides*, of Arizona and New Mexico, has toothless willow-shaped leaves and pointed acorns. The wood of the hophornbeam and American hornbeam is extremely hard, and these trees are sometimes called ironwoods. Knowlton hophornbeam, *Ostrya knowltonii*, of Arizona, southern Utah, and New Mexico, has leaves up to 2″ long and shorter clusters of fruits. Leaves of the sweet birch have a wintergreen aroma and taste. The bark resembles that of a cherry tree.

Page 72—Birches

The hard, heavy, handsomely grained wood of the yellow birch is used primarily for interior finishing and veneers. Water birch, *Betula occidentalis*, is a small tree scattered over the western half of North America. It has ovate leaves up to 2″ long and 1″ wide and "cones" about 1″ long that tend to hang from the branchlets. Because of their attractive bark, most birches make beautiful ornamentals. Weeping birch, *B. pendula*, an introduction from Europe, is a popular lawn tree. The leaves of the gray birch quiver in the wind like those of the quaking aspen.

Page 74—Alders, Horsetail Casuarina, Loblolly-bay, Basswoods

Speckled alder, *Alnus rugosa*, occurs all across Canada and the northeastern United States. It is a small tree with narrow leathery leaves and drooping woody "cones" about ½″ long. Arizona alder, *A. oblongifolia*, is a small tree with dark yellow-green leaves and drooping woody "cones" nearly 1″ long. Hazel alder, *A. serrulata*, another small tree of the eastern United States, has wavy-edged, fine-toothed leaves and erect woody "cones" up to ½″ long. The European alder, *A. glutinosa*, which has been introduced into North America, has nearly round leaves often broadly notched at the tip. Although the "cones" of the horsetail casuarina resemble the fruits of conifers, this species is actually a flowering plant. The trunk of the loblolly bay is distinctive because of its vertical red-brown fissures. Carolina basswood, *Tilia caroliniana*, of the southern United States, has leaves hairy but green on the lower surface.

Page 76—Tamarisk, Poplars

French tamarisk is sometimes grown as a novelty ornamental. Balm-of-Gilead, *Populus gileadensis*, is similar to the balsam poplar but has hairy leaves. It is of hybrid origin.

Page 78—Poplars

Eastern cottonwood is an exceedingly fast-growing tree that has gained some popularity as an ornamental. Lombardy poplar, *Populus nigra* var. *italica*, a tree with leaves similar to those of the eastern cottonwood, has a columnar growth form and was at one time highly desired as an ornamental, but it proves to be a fairly short-lived tree.

Page 80—Aspens, Willows

The flattened leaf stalks of the quaking and bigtooth aspens provide more surface area, so that the slightest wind causes the leaves to quiver. Quaking aspen has the broadest geographic range of any tree in North America. Both aspens are capable of forming dense stands by producing numerous suckers.

Black willow is the dominant willow of the eastern United States. Confined to the southeastern states are Coastal Plain willow, *Salix caroliniana*, with narrow leaves whitish on the lower surface, and Florida willow, *S. floridana*, with leaves 1½″–2″ wide. Shining willow, *S. lucida*, a tree with shiny, dark yellow-green leaves, grows in the northeastern United States, and satiny willow, *S. pellita*, with nearly toothless leaves, is found in the northern half of Maine and in New Hampshire, Vermont, New York, Michigan, Minnesota, and adjacent Canada. Willows occurring nearly all across the northern United States and Canada are pussy willow, *S. discolor*, with irregular, sparse teeth and leaf stalks ½″–1″ long; Bebb willow, *S. bebbiana*, with irregular, sparse teeth and leaf stalks less than ½″ long; meadow willow, *S. petiolaris*, with finely toothed leaves green on the lower surface; and balsam willow, *S. pyrifolia*, with finely toothed leaves paler on the lower surface.

Page 82—**Willows**

Crack willow is named for its very brittle branchlets. The flexible wood of the white and basket willows is ideal for making baskets. Scouler willow has the ability to colonize an area rapidly after a fire. Other willows, mostly found near the Pacific, are Hinds willow, *Salix hindsiana*, with no leaf stalks and leaves with few or no teeth; northwest willow, *S. sessilifolia*, with no leaf stalks and leaves finely toothed; Hooker willow, *S. hookeriana*, with stalked leaves widest about the middle and densely woolly below; Mackenzie willow, *S. mackenziana*, with stalked leaves widest above the middle and somewhat heart-shaped at the base; Sitka willow, *S. sitchensis*, with stalked leaves widest above the middle and without teeth; Tracy willow, *S. tracyi*, with stalked leaves widest above the middle and with few to several teeth; and river willow, *S. fluviatilis*, with stalked, lanceolate leaves widest near the base. In the southwest are yewleaf willow, *S. taxifolia*, with leaves less than ¼″ wide, and Bonpland willow, *S. bonplandiana*, with leaves at least ½″ wide. Several willows that do not attain tree stature are not included in this book.

Page 84—**Sourwood, Mountain-laurel, Madrones**

The leaves of the sourwood turn a brilliant scarlet in the autumn. A related plant in the southeastern United States is tree lyonia, *Lyonia ferruginea*, with wavy-edged, evergreen leaves. Flowers of the madrones are small and bell-shaped, usually either pink or white. Texas madrone, *Arbutus texana*, has leaves widest near the middle and dark red fruits.

Page 86—**Bumelias, Persimmon, Silverbells, Sweetleaf**

Bumelias usually have spines on their branchlets and produce their tiny flowers in clusters where the leaves are attached to the stem. Tough bumelia, *Bumelia tenax*, of the southern Atlantic coast, has rust-colored hairs on the lower surface of the leaves; saffron-plum, *B. celastrina*, of the southern tip of Texas and coastal southern Florida, has smooth, evergreen leaves. The fruit of the persimmon is edible after it has matured. Texas persimmon, *Diospyros texana*, has leaves only 1″–2″ long and black fruits. The lovely white bell-shaped flowers of the silverbells account for the trees' ornamental value. The sweet-tasting leaves account for the alternate common names of sweetleaf and horse sugar. The tree's small, fragrant flowers are produced before the leaves expand.

Page 88—**Cherries**

The fruits of chokecherry, black cherry, and pin cherry are valuable food for wildlife. Short, sharp, spine-like structures frequently grow from the branchlets of pin cherry. Other wild cherries are hollyleaf cherry, *Prunus ilicifolia*, of southern California, with spine-tipped teeth along the leaf edges; Catalina cherry, *P. lyonii*, of California's Channel Islands, with leaves bearing few or no teeth; and bitter cherry, *P. emarginata*, found mostly west of the Rocky Mountains, with irregular teeth along the leaf edges.

Page 90—**Plums, Mountain-ashes, Serviceberries, Crab Apple**

Several species of wild plums grow to be small trees. In Pennsylvania and adjacent states is the Allegheny plum, *Prunus alleghaniensis*, which has lanceolate leaves ¾″–1¼″ wide and red-purple fruits ½″–¾″ in diameter. Plums found primarily in the South and Southeast are Chickasaw plum, *P. angustifolia*, with lanceolate leaves less than 1″ wide and red or yellow plums ¼″–½″ in diameter, and flatwoods plum, *P. umbellata*, with leaves 1″–1½″ wide and nearly black plums ½″–1″ in diameter. From Louisiana and east Texas north to Nebraska and Missouri is the Mexican plum, *P. mexicana*, with leaves 1½″–2″ wide and purple fruits about ½″ long and slightly longer than they are wide. In the Midwest are wild goose plum, *P. munsoniana*, with leaves 2½″–4″ long, and hortulan plum, *P. hortulana*, with leaves 4″–6″ long. Klamath plum, *P. subcordata*, is confined to southern Oregon and California. It has very broad, nearly round leaves that are somewhat heart-shaped at the base. Related to the plums and cherries is the desert apricot, *P. fremontii*, of southern California. It has leaves only ½″–1¼″ long and yellow fruits about ½″ long. Mountain-ashes are sometimes grown as ornamentals, particularly the European mountain-ash, *Sorbus aucuparia*, which has very hairy leaflets. Sitka mountain-ash, *S. sitchensis*, native from Alaska to California, has fewer leaflets that are more coarsely toothed. Serviceberries, which are also called shadbushes, have fruits that are eaten by birds, squirrels, bears, and other animals. Western serviceberry, *Amelanchier alnifolia*, of the northwestern United States, western Canada, and Alaska, has ovate leaves 1″–1½″ wide; Utah serviceberry, *A. utahensis*, which grows in many western states, has nearly round leaves up to 1″ wide. Crab apples provide food for wildlife and can be made into jelly. Southern crab apple, *Malus angustifolia*, of the Southeast, has smooth, narrowly lanceolate leaves up to ½″ wide; sweet crab apple, *M. coronaria*, of the northeastern states, has smooth, ovate leaves ½″–1½″ wide; Oregon crab apple, *M. fusca*, has slightly hairy, broadly lanceolate leaves ½″–1½″ wide.

Page 92—Hawthorns, Catclaw Acacia, Silktree

Hawthorns are shrubs or small trees, particularly abundant in the eastern United States, where most of the species are exceptionally difficult to distinguish. Even most experts throw up their hands in despair. Western hawthorns are less confusing. The most common western species are black hawthorn, *Crataegus douglasii*, with short spines on the branchlets and blue-black fruits, and Columbia hawthorn, *C. columbiana*, with longer spines and red fruits. Catclaw acacia is one of many species in the genus *Acacia* that have spiny stems and numerous leaflets. Several are shrubs, and a few of the tree species are found only in the southern tips of Florida and Texas. Wright catclaw, *A. wrightii*, occurs throughout central Texas and is distinguished by its leaflets that are twice as large as those of the catclaw acacia. Silktree, a native of Asia, is grown as an ornamental in warmer regions of the United States.

Page 94—Mesquites, Redbud, Honeylocust, Coffeetree

Mesquite wood makes excellent firewood and imparts a delightful taste to foods cooked over it. The flowers attract honeybees, and the honey produced boasts an excellent flavor. Glandular mesquite, *Prosopis glandulosa*, has smooth leaves and flat fruit. The attractive flowers of the redbud make it a desirable ornamental. California redbud, *Cercus occidentalis*, has leathery leaves. Thornless variations of the honeylocust are sometimes grown as ornamentals. Waterlocust, *Gleditsia aquatica*, which occurs in swamps in the southern states, has pods only 1″–2″ long. Pioneers used to roast the seeds of the coffeetree and use them as a substitute for coffee beans.

Page 96—Paloverdes, Yellowwood, Mescalbean, Black Locust

Paloverdes are characterized by green twigs with a pair of spines at the base of each leaf. The hanging clusters of white flowers make the yellowwood a prized ornamental. Mescalbean is sometimes called coralbean because of the red seeds, which have narcotic properties. Texas sophora, *Sophora affinis*, has 13–15 leaflets per leaf. The large, showy flowers of most *Robinia* species make them popular as ornamentals. Some are shrubs. New Mexico locust, *R. neomexicana*, a small tree of the southwestern United States, has rose-colored flowers about 1″ long. Clammy locust, *R. viscosa*, found from Pennsylvania to Alabama, has rose-colored flowers about ¾″ long and leaflets with sticky hairs.

Page 98—Desert Ironwood, Bluegum, Dogwoods

Desert ironwood derives its name from its hard, strong wood. Bluegum is one of several hundred species of *Eucalyptus*, most of them native to Australia. Bluegum and a few others have been planted extensively in California and Florida for windbreaks. They are susceptible to temperatures that fall below

20°F. The showiness of the flowering dogwood and the Pacific dogwood when in flower is due not to the flowers themselves but to colorful, enlarged, petal-like structures called bracts, found at the base of each cluster of flowers. Several dogwoods that occur in North America are only shrubs. Dogwood berries provide food for many kinds of birds.

Page 100—Tupelo, Blackgum, Hollies

Water tupelo is codominant with baldcypress in many swamps in the southeastern United States. The leaves of the blackgum turn a brilliant red in the autumn. In addition to the American holly and large gallberry, other evergreen hollies, all native to the southeastern United States, are myrtle dahoon, *Ilex myrtifolia*, with toothless leaves; dahoon, *I. cassine*, with leaves that are 1½"–4" long and have some sharp teeth; and yaupon, *I. vomitoria*, with leaves that are ½"–1½" long and have some rounded teeth. Several deciduous hollies that may grow to be small trees also live in the southeastern United States. They are mountain winterberry, *I. montana*, with leaves that are smooth on the lower surface and mostly 3" long or longer; Carolina holly, *I. ambigua*, with leaves that are smooth on the lower surface and less than 3" long; smooth winterberry, *I. laevigata*, with leaves that are hairy only on the veins on the lower surface; common winterberry, *I. verticillata*, with leaves that are densely hairy on the lower surface and tapering at the base; and Sarvis holly, *I. amelanchier*, with leaves that are finely hairy on the lower surface and rounded at the base.

Page 102—Buckthorn, Raintree, Soapberry, Buckeyes

There are several species of *Rhamnus* in North America, but most of them are shrubs rather than trees. However, in the Pacific Northwest cascara buckthorn, *R. purshiana*, may reach a height of 40'. Golden raintree is a fast-growing species native to Asia and first grown in North America as an ornamental more than 200 years ago. The fruits of the soapberries, when rubbed vigorously in water, will produce a lather. Wingleaf soapberry, *Sapindus saponaria*, of southeastern Georgia and Florida, has an even number of leaflets. The Ohio buckeye sometimes may have 7 leaflets rather than 5. Other buckeyes in the southern and southeastern United States, none of which have sticky buds, are painted buckeye, *Aesculus sylvatica*, with pink or creamy yellow flowers, and red buckeye, *A. pavia*, with red flowers.

Page 104—Horsechestnut, Maples

The large clusters of white flowers account for the ornamental value of the horsechestnut, a tree native to southeastern Europe. Like the horsechestnut, the California buckeye, *Aesculus californica*, has sticky buds, but the husks of its fruits are without spines. The wood of the bigleaf maple is used for furniture and cabinets. Striped maple gets its common name from the vertical white lines on the young green bark.

Page 106—**Maples**

The leaves of Rocky Mountain maple and bigtooth maple turn a brilliant orange-red in the autumn. Those of red maple may turn red or yellow in the autumn. Silver maple is sometimes called soft maple; unlike that of the sugar maple, its wood is not valuable. Black maple, which is closely related to sugar maple, yields maple syrup.

Page 108—**Maples, Sumacs**

Sugar maple leaves usually turn a brilliant orange-red in the autumn. Maple syrup can be tapped from the trunks of the trees, and the wood is valuable for furniture and cabinets. Chalk maple, *Acer leucoderme*, and Florida maple, *A. barbatum*, both occur in the southeastern United States. The bark of the chalk maple is white; that of the Florida maple is darker. The leaves of smooth sumac and shining sumac turn a bright red early in the autumn. Several other sumacs in North America usually grow as shrubs. Some that may become small trees are lemonade sumac, *Rhus integrifolia*, of southern California, with simple, evergreen leaves pointed at the tip; sugar sumac, *R. ovata*, of the southwestern United States, with simple, evergreen leaves rounded at the tip; and prairie sumac, *R. lanceolata*, of Texas and adjacent states, with deciduous, pinnately compound leaves with leaflets that are up to ½″ wide and attached to a winged stalk. Poison sumac, *Toxicodendron vernix*, a small tree found in the eastern half of North America, has alternate, deciduous, pinnately compound leaves that are poisonous to the touch. It has white berries. Related to the sumacs is American smoketree, *Cotinus obovatus*, of the southern United States. It has simple, alternate, deciduous leaves with slightly wavy edges.

Page 110—**Ailanthus, Prickly-ash, Chinaberry, Devils-walkingstick**

Ailanthus, sometimes called tree of heaven, is native to Asia. The leaflets often have a disagreeable odor. The oil produced by the leaves of the prickly-ash was used by the pioneers to relieve toothache. Hercules-club, *Zanthoxylum clava-herculis*, which occurs in the southern United States and along the Atlantic Coastal Plain from Maryland to Florida, has leaflets regularly toothed along the margins. Chinaberry is native to Asia. Its berries are poisonous if eaten. Because of its rapid growth, chinaberry is cultivated as an ornamental in warmer parts of North America. The berries of the devils-walkingstick are eaten by animals, particularly cedar waxwings.

Page 112—**Oleander, Devilwood, Fringetree, Swamp-privet**

Oleander is native to the Mediterranean area but is planted extensively in warmer regions of the world because of its attractive flowers. Its milky sap is poisonous. Fruits of the devilwood provide food for wildlife. The large clusters of white flowers of the fringetree make it an attractive ornamental. The clusters of small yellow flowers of the swamp-privet bloom before the leaves appear in early spring. Desert-olive forestiera, *Forestiera phillyreoides*, of southern Arizona, has hairy leaves less than ½″ wide; Texas forestiera, *F. angustifolia*, has smooth leaves less than ½″ wide; Florida-privet, *F. segregata*, of Georgia and Florida, has leaves ½″–1″ wide.

Page 114—**Ashes**

A variation of green ash with densely hairy branchlets and lower leaf surfaces is called red ash. The wood of several species of ash is used for making baseball bats, oars, and tool handles. The seeds are eaten by many kinds of wildlife. Ashes with a more limited geographic range in the United States are Carolina ash, *Fraxinus caroliniana*, of the southeastern states, with 5–7 sharply toothed leaflets and fruits 1¼″–2¼″ long and ½″–¾″ wide; fragrant ash, *F. cuspidata*, of Arizona, New Mexico, and Texas, with 3–7 very narrow, toothed, smooth leaflets and fruits ½″–1″ long and ¼″–½″ wide; two-petal ash, *F. dipetala*, of California, with 3–7 narrow, toothed, smooth leaflets and narrow fruits ¾″–1¼″ long and ¼″ wide; Texas ash, *F. texensis*, of Texas and southern Oklahoma, with 5 broad, nearly toothless, round-tipped leaflets and fruits ¾″–1″ long and ¼″ wide; velvet ash, *F. velutina*, of the southwestern United States, with 3–5 shallowly toothed, densely hairy leaflets and fruits ½″–1″ long and ¼″ wide; Berlandier ash, *F. berlandierana*, of southern Texas, with 3–5 narrow, pointed, toothed, smooth leaflets and fruits 1¼″–1½″ long and ¼″ wide; Chihuahua ash, *F. papillosa*, of southern Arizona and New Mexico, with 7–9 narrow leaflets warty and hairy on the lower surface and fruits 1″–1½″ long and ¼″ wide; Gregg ash, *F. greggii*, of southwestern Texas, with 3–7 oblanceolate, nearly toothless leaflets and fruits ½″–¾″ long and ¼″ wide; Goodding ash, *F. gooddingii*, of southern Arizona, with 5–7 nearly evergreen oblanceolate leaflets and fruits ½″–¾″ long and ¼″ wide; and Oregon ash, *F. latifolia*, of the Pacific states, with 5–7 broadly lanceolate, shallowly toothed leaflets hairy on the lower surface and fruits 1″–2″ long and ¼″–½″ wide. Singleleaf ash, *F. anomala*, of the southwestern United States, is unusual among the ashes in having simple leaves.

Page 116—**Ash, Paulownia, Catalpa, Desert-willow**

The large clusters of lavender flowers account for the ornamental value of the royal paulownia, which is also known as princess tree. Southern catalpa, *Catalpa bignonioides*, found in Mississippi, Alabama, Georgia, and northern Florida, has smaller flowers than does northern catalpa. It is sometimes grown as an ornamental, as is the desert-willow.

Page 118—**Viburnums, Palms**

The fruits of the viburnums are eaten by wildlife. Nannyberry, *Viburnum lentago*, of the northern states and Canada, has toothed leaves more pointed at the tip than those of the blackhaw. Walter viburnum, *V. obovatum*, of the southeastern United States, has evergreen leaves with few or no teeth. The coconut palm is found along ocean shores in tropical parts of the world. The coconut has high food value and produces a valuable oil. Texas palmetto, *Sabal texana*, may grow to a height of 50'. California washingtonia, *Washingtonia filifera*, of southern California and adjacent Arizona, has fan-shaped leaves and prickly leaf stalks. Several other palms are native to the southern tip of Florida, including the Florida Keys.

Studying Trees

For the most part, trees can be studied well—at least at the beginning level—with few aids other than this book and an interest in trees. We believe, however, that you will find the following items handy: a hand lens, a pocketknife, a small plastic bag, and a notebook. Indeed, we regard the first of these as a necessity. On occasion, you may also wish for binoculars. Further, you may wish to assemble your own herbarium, a collection of pressed and dried specimens of the trees you are learning to identify.

Hand lens. In general, a hand lens bears about the same relationship to the study of trees as do binoculars to the study of birds or a telescope to the study of celestial objects: although the objects of study can sometimes be seen without such an aid, they can be seen much better with one. There are instances in which a hand lens is not merely helpful but essential—for example, when you want to tell whether a juniper tree has smooth-edged or jagged-edged scale-leaves.

The best kind of lens to use has a magnifying power of at least 10 (10 ×). To use a hand lens with maximum efficiency, follow this procedure. First, bring the lens *up to* within an inch or an inch and a half from your eye. (The usual tendency for people unused to such an aid is to hold the lens about a foot away from their eye.) Then slowly bring the specimen *up to* the lens until it comes into focus. Be certain that the specimen is receiving the maximum amount of light possible; do not block the light with your head (another common error), thus putting the specimen in a shadow. You should now be able to see well all that the lens can reveal.

A hand lens, being small, is rather easily lost. The best way to avoid such loss and to have the lens handily available is to hang it around your neck on a piece of strong, smooth twine 3 to 3½ feet long (or on shoelaces tied together to make this length). Keep the lens closed when it is not in use. Should it get dirty—and it will—clean it carefully with a facial tissue. Use as little pressure as possible on the glass.

Pocketknife. While there are many kinds of trees whose small twigs can be easily broken clean from the branch for use as study specimens, there are others, such as elms, in which a whole strip of bark may come off with the twig. To avoid such damage to the tree, we suggest that you use a pocketknife—a sharp one—to cut off your study twig carefully and cleanly. (Remember that in some areas, such as national parks, you should not cut *anything* from trees.) Pruning shears, though bulkier than a pocketknife, work well, too.

Small plastic bag. A plastic bag of the size used in the kitchen for garbage (or even somewhat smaller) is a convenient container in which to bring your specimens back to camp or home for further study. Some people prefer to do *all* of their study in a place other than by the tree from which they collected the specimen. (We are less than enthusiastic about this method, feeling that the tree should be "at hand." But we recognize that rain, or perhaps an overabundance of mosquitoes, may sometimes make it necessary.) Study specimens carried in a plastic bag should last well enough for a day or so if the bag is kept out of the sun, if it is not kept in a closed, hot car, and if the specimens in it have been lightly sprinkled with water (do not flood them). They keep well in a refrigerator. If the bag contains more than one or two specimens, do not rely on your memory to "keep them straight." Each should be labeled with a number that corresponds to a number in your notebook (see below). Use a piece of heavy paper (for example, half of a 3″ × 5″ card); write, in *pencil,* the number on the paper; cut or tear a small slot in the center of the paper; and, finally, insert the bottom of the twig into the slot. Your specimen is now labeled.

Notebook. A pocket-size notebook is good to have so that you may record various data about the tree you are studying: bark features, height, diameter, flower color, fruit characteristics, and so on. Do *not* rely on your memory for these data. Write with a pencil to avoid the smudging that may result from ink should the book get damp. Data for each tree should be numbered, and you should assign consecutive numbers to consecutive trees.

Binoculars. Binoculars are sometimes handy in tree study when you want to see fruits or cones that may be out of reach. For example, fir cones many feet above the ground are often most easily seen in this way. Of course, you may climb the fir if you wish, but you probably will get resin from the bark onto your clothes and your hands.

Herbarium. We suggest that for future reference, you may want to press and dry leafy twigs of the various kinds of trees you have identified. Such a collection of specimens is called a herbarium. (Your grandmother made use of this technique when she pressed and dried flowers between pages of a book.) Such specimens are fine—and free—mementoes of the places in which you have seen trees, and they help you recall or review what you have learned about the trees. Preparing them is easy.

The leafy twig you select for pressing and drying should be average in appearance and not partly eaten by insects or otherwise damaged. It should be of such a size that, when pressed, it will fit comfortably into an area about 15″ high and 10″ wide. If the specimen has so many leaves that if it is pressed as is, a jumbled mass will result, simply cut or pinch off some of the leaves, leaving the base of the leaf stalks to show where the leaves were. This specimen should be placed in a folded half-sheet of newspaper (not larger than 12″ × 15″ when folded). The newspaper should be numbered on its long, outer margin, the number corresponding to the number of an entry in the notebook in which you record field data. Be certain that some leaves show their upper side and some their lower.

Of the various ways to accomplish pressing and drying, the easiest is simply to place the specimen with its newspaper sheet between two entire sections of newspaper. Then place all the material on the floor and put several books on it. The weight of the books will press the specimen flat, and the moisture in the specimen will be drawn into the surrounding paper. Several specimens, each between newspaper sections, may be pressed in a stack this way. Change the newspaper sheets and sections daily, setting the damp ones aside to dry for use another day. Specimens from most broad-leaved trees will dry in a few days; those from scale-leaved or needle-leaved trees (conifers) may take a week or more. The specimen is dry if a leaf breaks when it is bent (press an extra leaf or two with the specimen for this test).

The data for the collection can be typed or printed neatly on a 3″ × 5″ card, which can be paper-clipped to the sheet in which you pressed the specimen and in which it can be stored. To be most useful, the data should include at least the name of the tree, a description of the kind of place the tree was growing (for example, *pine forest, swamp, fencerow, old field*), data on tree height and trunk diameter, the location of the tree (for example, *3 miles S.E. of Oakville, Elm Co., Ill.*), the date, and your name as collector.

If you wish, each of your pressed and dried specimens can be mounted, that is, glued to a sheet of heavy white paper cut to 16.5″ × 11.5″. Suitable paper can be purchased at an art-supply store; a household white glue is quite satisfactory. First, glue the label to the lower right-hand corner of the sheet. Then decide which arrangement of the specimen on the sheet suits you best, especially which side of the specimen you want to be "up." Next turn the specimen over and apply *small* drops of glue at intervals over its back. Put the specimen, glue side down, back onto the sheet; cover it with a sheet of waxed paper. Finally, place some books on top of the waxed paper to be certain the specimen lies flat as the glue dries. Let the specimen remain undisturbed for several hours. The mount will then be finished. If reinforcing appears necessary, narrow strips of glue or of plastic or cloth tape (*not* scotch tape) can be put over leaf stalks and stems to help affix them well.

If you are a teacher, remember that such mounted specimens are excellent teaching aids.

Because various kinds of insects may feed on and destroy dried plant specimens, the specimens should be stored in a plastic bag in which a few moth crystals are scattered. Handling a stack of specimens will be easier if it is placed between cardboards cut to the size of the folded newspaper sheets.

Further Reading

Atlas of United States Trees. Vol. 1: Conifers and Important Hardwoods. Elbert L. Little, Jr. Washington, D.C.: U.S. Dept. of Agriculture, 1971 (Miscellaneous Publication No. 1146).

Atlas of United States Trees. Vol. 2: Alaska Trees and Common Shrubs. Leslie A. Viereck and Elbert L. Little, Jr. Washington, D.C.: U.S. Dept. of Agriculture, 1975 (Miscellaneous Publication No. 1293).

Atlas of United States Trees. Vol. 3: Minor Western Hardwoods. Elbert L. Little, Jr. Washington, D.C.: U.S. Dept. of Agriculture, 1976 (Miscellaneous Publication No. 1134).

Atlas of United States Trees. Vol. 4: Minor Eastern Hardwoods. Elbert L. Little, Jr. Washington, D.C.: U.S. Dept. of Agriculture, 1977 (Miscellaneous Publication No. 1342).

Atlas of United States Trees. Vol. 5: Florida. Elbert L. Little, Jr. Washington, D.C.: U.S. Dept. of Agriculture, 1978 (Miscellaneous Publication No. 1361).

Atlas of United States Trees. Vol. 6: Supplement. Elbert L. Little, Jr. Washington, D.C.: U.S. Dept. of Agriculture, 1981 (Miscellaneous Publication No. 1410).

Audubon Society Field Guide to North American Trees: Eastern Region. Elbert L. Little. New York: Knopf, 1980.

Audubon Society Field Guide to North American Trees: Western Region. Elbert L. Little. New York: Knopf, 1980.

Checklist of United States Trees (Native and Naturalized). Elbert L. Little, Jr. Washington, D.C.: U.S. Dept. of Agriculture, 1979 (Agriculture Handbook 41).

Complete Trees of North America Field Guide and Natural History. Thomas S. Elias. New York: Outdoor Life/Nature Books, 1980.

Forest Trees of the Pacific Slope. George B. Sudworth. New York: Dover, 1967. (Reprint of 1908 edition.)

Knowing Your Trees. George Harris Collingwood and Warren D. Brush (rev. and ed. by Devereux Butcher). Washington, D.C.: American Forestry Association, 1965.

Manual of Cultivated Conifers. Gerd Krüssmann. Portland, Ore.: Timber Press, 1985.

Native Trees of Canada, 8th ed. Ottawa: Environment Canada, 1979 (Publication 45-61-1979).

Natural History of Trees of Eastern and Central North America. Donald Curloss Peattie. Boston: Houghton Mifflin, 1950.

Natural History of Western Trees. Donald Curloss Peattie. Boston: Houghton Mifflin, 1953.

Northwest Conifers: A Photographic Key. Dale N. Bever. Portland, Ore.: Binford and Mort, 1981.

Textbook of Dendrology, 6th ed. William M. Harlow, E. S. Harrar, and F. M. White. New York: McGraw-Hill, 1979.

Trees and Shrubs of the United States: A Bibliography for Identification. Elbert L. Little, Jr., and Barbara H. Honkala. Washington, D.C.: U.S. Dept. of Agriculture, 1976 (Miscellaneous Publication 1336).

Glossary

See also the illustrations of hardwood leaf shapes in the front of the book.

ALTERNATE—denoting an arrangement of leaves in which the leaves are not situated directly across from each other along the stem (*compare* OPPOSITE)

ANGIOSPERM—a plant whose reproductive structures are flowers rather than cones (*compare* GYMNOSPERM); also called a hardwood

BRACT—in conifers, one of the many pointed, papery structures that protrude from among the scales of the cones of the western larches, some firs, and Douglas-firs; in hardwoods, a structure at the base of a flower, often more or less leaf-like in appearance

BRANCHLET—a small branch

BROADLEAF TREE—a tree with leaves that are broad and flat, as opposed to needle-like or scale-like

COMPOUND—said of a leaf that is divided into leaflets (*compare* SIMPLE)

CONIFER—a woody plant whose reproductive structures are not flowers but usually cones; a member of the gymnosperm group

DECIDUOUS—said of a tree whose leaves die and usually fall off at the end of the growing season

DOUBLY PINNATE—twice divided into segments

ELLIPTICAL—broadest at the middle, tapering equally to either end

ENTIRE—said of a leaf whose edges are smooth, not jagged

EVERGREEN—said of leaves that persist on the plant throughout the winter

GYMNOSPERM—a plant whose reproductive structures are not flowers but usually cones (*compare* ANGIOSPERM); also called a softwood

HARDWOOD—a tree whose reproductive structures are flowers rather than cones; an angiosperm

LANCEOLATE—lance-shaped; broadest near the base, gradually tapering to the tip

LEAFLET—one unit of a compound leaf

LEAF SCAR—the mark left on a twig after a leaf falls

LOBED—said of a leaf whose edges have notches larger than teeth

MIDVEIN—the central vein of a leaf

OBLANCEOLATE—reverse in shape from lanceolate, that is, lance-shaped but broadest at the tip and tapering toward the base

OPPOSITE—denoting an arrangement of leaves in which the leaves are situated directly across from each other along the stem (*compare* ALTERNATE)

OVATE—broadly rounded at the base, becoming narrowed above; broader than lanceolate

PALMATE—arranged radiately, like the fingers of a hand

PINNATE—divided once into distinct segments

RESIN DUCT—in conifers, one of the minute, resin-filled, drinking-straw-like tubes running lengthwise in the leaves of certain species

SHRUB—a woody plant with several stems of more or less uniform size arising from ground level

SIMPLE—said of a leaf that is not divided into leaflets (*compare* COMPOUND)

SOFTWOOD—a tree whose reproductive structures are not flowers but usually cones; a gymnosperm

TOOTHED—having jagged edges

TREE—a woody plant usually having a single stem and attaining a height of at least 20′

WHORLED—said of leaves or flowers in which three or more are attached equidistant from each other and at the same level on a stem

WING—a thin, flat outgrowth from a seed, fruit, or stem

Index

Page numbers in boldface refer to species descriptions accompanied by an illustration.

About the Authors

ROBERT H. MOHLENBROCK is Distinguished Professor of Botany at Southern Illinois University at Carbondale, where he has taught since 1957. A Fellow of the Illinois State Academy of Science, he is the author of more than 30 books on botanical subjects, including ten volumes in the series *The Illustrated Flora of Illinois* (Southern Illinois University Press). He serves as a consultant to the U.S. Forest Service and the Illinois Department of Conservation. In 1986, Professor Mohlenbrock was named North American chairman for botany of the Species Survival Commission of the International Union of Conservation of Nature and Natural Resources. Since 1984 he has written a monthly column on the national forests of the United States for the magazine *Natural History*.

JOHN W. THIERET is Professor of Botany at Northern Kentucky University. Well-known as a botanist and editor, he is the author of *Louisiana Ferns and Fern Allies* (Louisiana Natural History Museum, 1980) and coauthor of *Aquatic and Wetland Plants of Kentucky* (Kentucky Nature Preserves Commission, 1987). He serves as editor of the journal *Economic Botany* and associate editor of the journal *Sida*. He is also on the editorial boards of the major series *Vascular Flora of Southeastern United States* and *Flora of North America*. Professor Thieret's botanical field work has taken him throughout the United States as well as to Canada, Mexico, and the West Indies. A popular speaker, he is in great demand as a leader of botanical field trips for both amateurs and professionals.

About the Artist

HOWARD S. FRIEDMAN is widely known for his work in scientific illustration, particularly in the field of natural history. He has contributed illustrations of nature subjects for projects of the American Museum of Natural History. His works have appeared in numerous books, encyclopedias, and magazines.

Other books in the authoritative, highly popular
Macmillan Field Guide Series
are available at your local bookstore or by mail.
To order directly, return the coupon below to

MACMILLAN PUBLISHING COMPANY
Special Sales Department
866 Third Avenue
New York, New York 10022

Line Sequence	ISBN	Author/Title	Price	Quantity
1	0020796501	Dunlop: **ASTRONOMY**, paperback	$ 8.95	_____
2	002063370X	Moody: **FOSSILS**, paperback	$ 8.95	_____
3	0020796404	Bell/Wright: **ROCKS AND MINERALS**, paperback	$ 8.95	_____
4	0020796609	Bull: **BIRDS OF NORTH AMERICA**, paperback	$ 9.95	_____
5	0025182307	Bull: **BIRDS OF NORTH AMERICA**, hardcover	$19.95	_____
6	002063420X	Mohlenbrock: **WILDFLOWERS**, paperback	$ 9.95	_____
7	0025854402	Mohlenbrock: **WILDFLOWERS**, hardcover	$24.95	_____
8	0020137001	Dunlop: **WEATHER AND FORECASTING**, paperback	$ 8.95	_____
9	0020636903	Bessette/Sundberg: **MUSHROOMS**, paperback	$12.95	_____
10	0026152606	Bessette/Sundberg: **MUSHROOMS**, hardcover	$24.95	_____
11	0020634307	Mohlenbrock/Thieret: **TREES**, paperback	$12.95	_____
12	0025854607	Mohlenbrock/Thieret: **TREES**, hardcover	$24.95	_____

Sub-total $ _____

Please add postage and handling costs—$1.00 for the first book
and 50¢ for each additional book $ _____

Total $ _____

_____Enclosed is my check/money order payable to Macmillan Publishing Co.

_____Bill my_____MasterCard_____Visa Card #_____

Expiration date_____Signature_____

—Charge orders valid only with signature

Control No. [   ]   Order Type [Reg]   Lines [   ]   Units

Ship to:_____   Bill to:_____

_____   _____

_____   _____

_____Zip Code   _____Zip Code

For information regarding bulk purchases, please write to Special Sales Director at the above address. Publisher's prices are subject to change without notice. Offer good May 1, 1987, through December 31, 1988. Allow 3 weeks for delivery.   FC# 611

Field Notes